"*Final Passage* is no mere recounting of case studies of the dying process. Rather, it is the lived experience of a compassionate, understanding and truly loving caregiver. Barbara Harris Whitfield shares her most intimate thoughts and emotions in this engaging account of human relationships, which demonstrate the unmistakable bonds connecting all of us to each other and to our Divine Source.

"*Final Passage* should be required reading for all health professionals who care for the terminally ill, from physicians to counselors, from nurses to orderlies."

—Jack McBride
executive director, Shepherd's Gate Hospice, Inc.
Covington, Georgia

"*Final Passage* will help families of patients facing death, and health-care professionals who see death as failure, to understand and comfort the dying without interfering with the natural process. Barbara Whitfield shows us how dying can be an opportunity to explore and deepen our spiritual dimension. This book will help us be 'real' not only at the deathbed but every day of our lives, so that we will not die without having first lived."

—Bruce Greyson, M.D.
professor of psychiatry, University of Virginia
and editor, *Journal of Near-Death Studies*

FINAL PASSAGE

Sharing the Journey as This Life Ends

Barbara Harris Whitfield

Health Communications, Inc.
Deerfield Beach, Florida
www.hci-online.com

To contact the author, send a SASE to:
Barbara Harris Whitfield
P.O. Box 420487
Atlanta, GA 30342
email: c-bwhit@mindspring.com

For the location of a hospice near you, call the National Hospice
Organization at 800-658-8898.

Library of Congress Cataloging-in-Publication Data

Whitfield, Barbara Harris, date.
    Final passage : sharing the journey as this life ends / Barbara Harris
Whitfield.
        p. cm.
    Includes bibliographical references and index.
    ISBN 1-55874-540-8 (trade pbk.)
    1. Near-death experiences. 2. Near-death experiences—Religious
aspects. 3. Death—Psychological aspects. I. Title.
BF1045.N4W45   1998
155.9'37—dc21   97-45630
                                                  CIP

Publisher: Health Communications, Inc.
3201 S.W. 15th Street
Deerfield Beach, Florida 33442-8190

Cover design by Lawna Patterson Oldfield

This book is dedicated with love
in memory of
Julius and Florence Silverman
and
Jim and May Doherty

Contents

Acknowledgments

I want to thank everyone described in these stories. These people freely gave of their time and their hearts. Without them sharing their truth with me, I could never have written this book.

I would like to give a special acknowledgment and thank you from the bottom of my heart to Mary Ellen Doherty Layden and David Doherty. I also want to thank my brother, Marshall Silverman, for his help and for just being who he is.

Several of my friends and relatives read this manuscript and gave me encouragement—more than once. Thank you to Eunice Silverman, Jackie Whitfield, Anne Beaver, Robynne Moran, Robin and Steve Harris, Sarah Harris, Kimberly Dudzinski, Bruce Greyson, Jack McBride, Chuck Darlington, Jane Miller and JoAnn Chambers. I also want to say thank you to Al Sullivan, Diane Mann and Paul Furgalack.

Nina Diamond worked with me early on—coaxing me and editing the proposal. She helped me to bring out memories that were buried in my heart. She showed me how to take the essence and give it words. I cannot thank her enough for her help and encouragement.

Christine Belleris and Matthew Diener, at Health Communications, Inc., are always wonderful to work with. Christine not

only encouraged me to start this book, she gave me the struc-
ture I needed to create it. Matthew is always there patiently
helping in any and every way he can. His expertise is remarkable. Lisa Drucker patiently assisted the editorial process and
graciously gave me encouragement and feedback. Nancy
Burke, my out-of-house editor, did a wonderful job of helping
me to make my words clear. Working with everyone else at
Health Communications—the entire staff—was and is a joy.

I also want to thank my husband, Charles Whitfield, for his
loving patience and for his gentle expertise.

And last, I want to thank Spirit for the opportunities I have
been given so I could write this book.

Introduction

The only real pain
When we die
Is if we do it
Without living first

                                        —BHW

Most people believe death is frightening, painful and final.
In this book I will share with you my experiences as a witness
to the dying process. I will show you how we can give comfort and witness without changing or interfering with what is
happening naturally.

Years ago, I worked in the labor and delivery rooms of several hospitals. The birthing process and the dying process are
similar. Just as an expectant mother in labor is totally involved
with every feeling her body produces, the dying are totally
involved with their bodies, processing every physical feeling
and drifting off between the pains and distress. Those who
assist an expectant mother through labor and birth are totally
involved, too. We who attend the dying, who assist in the
death process, are also totally involved. This intense focus
deepens the spiritual dimensions of both being born and
dying.

In my work as a researcher I have interviewed hundreds of
people who have had near-death experiences (NDEs).
Occasionally, I interview women who have also had the experience we call "near-death," but their experience happened in
childbirth, and they were not experiencing any physical dif-
ficulties that threatened their lives. They were, however, in
touch with the same spiritual consciousness that is reported
by people as they are dying. Souls are birthed into this life and
then eventually souls leave. If we remain more aware during
birth and death, we can turn up the volume in our hearts'
ability to perceive this spiritual dimension. When we enter
this life we are surrounded by caring and love. We deserve
caring and love again when this life ends.*

SPIRITUAL GROWTH

Every time I assist a dying patient, I grow spiritually. I have
gained so much from these dear people. When they are open
to death and when their families are open, we share a deep
spiritual experience, not only with one another, but also with
the great spiritual energy of the universe. We speak of Spirit's
presence (Holy Spirit, Christ consciousness, Buddha nature,
or whatever you choose to call it) behind closed doors at hospice meetings. Until recently, academics have not addressed
this spiritual energy and then only in the most removed set-
tings. Sometimes orthodox religion confuses us by placing
this spiritual presence somewhere between our belief in Santa
Claus and in angels. But recently we have again embraced our
natural birthright to acknowledge and experience the realm of

* Hospice of the Western Reserve, Cleveland, Ohio.

Spirit in this world. It feels as though the veil between this reality and the reality of Spirit has become thinner—more transparent and easier to access. Perhaps this is why more and more people are acknowledging a strong belief in God or a great spiritual energy, in angels, and in the afterlife.

These stories in *Final Passage* are true, and each one contains its own unique wisdom that gradually opens the reader spiritually—just as the people in the stories opened.

For the growing number of people who are now preparing for and coping with their parents' deaths, and for young people who perhaps have never experienced a loved one's death, this book will prepare them. For healthcare professionals who have been unable to handle their patients' deaths, for physicians who feel like failures each time a patient dies, and for people—and their families—who are facing death in the near future, this book will assist them in understanding and relating to the dying process.

I share these stories, and what I have learned, to help others accept death—and the journey of life and death—more easily and see the connection to Spirit that is at the heart of the dying process.

Each time I participate in the death of a loved one, a client or a patient, the kindness of others overwhelms me. I show in these stories how it is possible to be present, offering kindness and stability, and how the kindness and the compassion spread. Sometimes the dying person becomes a beacon of Light, and the Light softens those attending the death, regardless of their previous beliefs, and transforms them. They feel compelled to share their new way of being with others. And though the dying person may leave us behind, they leave us with a new life. They become a living part of us.

When Sherry Rosen (the person in chapter 2) died, I was

asked to speak at her memorial service. She was only forty-eight years old when I assisted in her death, and in the last week of her life she left an amazing legacy to her family, friends and me. It was a legacy of *how* we can experience death. Whether we ourselves are dying, or we are attending someone else's death, we can do so with more awareness and compassion. When we do, honesty, or being real, underlies every moment of the dying process because our realness and compassion leave room for the truth to emerge. Compassion accepts painful as well as joyful memories. There is no judgment in compassion, so the dying person can act and be totally real. The old saying "The truth shall set us free" is especially poignant as we prepare to die. Honesty with self, others and God at any stage of life sets us free. As we die, "sharing our truth" gives us our last chance to be free of the inertia we made in this life. Sharing our truth sets us free to be real. It is only when we are real that we can experientially feel our connection to God and Spirit before we die.

DYING AS A PROCESS

It is hard to find a precise "moment" of death. Death is a process, as each of these stories will demonstrate. "Process" gives us room for communion and peace, joy and tears, loss and growth. While the body may shut down in just a few hours or even moments, the soul's journey involves a slower process. Supported by loved ones and caregivers, the soul reviews this lifetime and prepares for the future. By surrendering to the process, loved ones and caregivers can receive much in return: healing, comfort and closure.

A hospice nurse who had often visited Sherry came to her house shortly after she died and asked me what I had done.

The nurse had sensed something different surrounding Sherry's death in the reactions of the family and in the way things were handled. "Please tell me what you did," she requested. "I know there's something missing in my work and I feel that what's missing is *here.*"

At the time I couldn't give her a brief analytical description about what happens when I attend people as they die. Hopefully the stories in this book will answer some of her questions. I share these experiences of my attending the dying process from my vantage point as both a thanatologist (someone who studies death and dying) and a near-death experiencer (NDEr). As an NDEr, I have witnessed and experienced death firsthand. Most NDErs are not afraid to die. Indeed, most of us look forward to going back, although not before we've done all the things we want to do first.

UNIVERSAL ENERGY

When I trained as a massage therapist, I was able to synthesize the training I received doing massage and energy work with my earlier respiratory therapy training.

This experiential knowledge enhanced my understanding of the energy arousal that occurs during an NDE. I had sensed during my own NDEs, and now understand, that this intelligent energy of our soul does not die when our bodies die. It is released into the universe. And if we don't die, as happens in the NDE, then the energy makes itself known to us and helps us grow. In this book I speak as both a clinician and a researcher who understands what is universal to NDErs and to dying patients. I am also speaking as a healer and spiritual guide who feels a connection with my dying patients and with the universal energy that guides us all. Much of my last book, *Spiritual Awakenings: Insights of the Near-Death Experience and*

Other Doorways to Our Soul, was about what I refer to as divine or universal energy, also known as Holy Spirit, Ruach Ha Kodesh, Kundalini, and other names.

In 1981, I met Kenneth Ring, Ph.D., a professor of psychology at the University of Connecticut. We talked at the first conference I attended on NDEs. I told him about my two experiences while suspended in a Stryker-frame circle bed after spinal surgery, and I told him about the experiences of my patients, too. In 1982, Dr. Ring interviewed me for his second book, *Heading Toward Omega: In Search of the Meaning of the Near-Death Experience*. This book became a classic in the field of near-death studies because of its theory that this divine or universal energy is awakened or aroused in deep spiritual experiences, which Dr. Ring refers to as "core experiences."

My experiences and my subsequent life changes, including energy arousal, became a key topic in *Heading Toward Omega*. Later, I became a researcher in the field of near-death studies. During that time, Ken Ring, Bruce Greyson and I showed in several studies that there is an energy arousal, which we call the "Physio-Kundalini Syndrome." People who have had a deep spiritual or core experience triggered by being near death, in childbirth, in deep prayer or meditation, and the like, report experiencing this syndrome. My second book, *Spiritual Awakenings* goes into depth on the triggers and the energy arousal.

Over the years, since my colleagues and I first described this syndrome, we have joined the international group of researchers called the Kundalini Research Network to discuss and share our findings on this universal energy. We have conducted numerous research studies in this new scientific area, one that until recently had been relegated to the esoteric and occult branches of religion.

As Eastern science makes us more aware of this universal energy's importance in health, our attitudes are slowly changing in Western medicine. They are also changing because of the near-death studies research that has demonstrated this energy's activation during the dying process. I have participated in this research both as a researcher and as a subject. Because of this unique background, I wrote *Final Passage* from the perspective of how important universal energy is on many levels: in helping spiritual growth, in reducing pain and in creating a healing atmosphere. And while there can be no "cure" in death, there can certainly be a kind of "healing." And healing is not only for the dying person, but for family, friends and significant others.

My unique experience of the death process has helped me create a new knowledge about how to touch people safely as they die and about how to work with the unique energy that surrounds the dying process. Since the mid-1980s I have taught hospice workshops. At first, I wasn't allowed to talk about physical touch. It is only in the last few years that hospices and hospitals have begun to recognize the need for physical touch. Because of my direct experience of the first few stages of dying, my continuing participation in the research of spiritual energy arousal, and my clinical background as a respiratory therapist and massage therapist, in this book I am able to share not only the techniques of safe touch but also other unique and simple ways to work with the dying. However, there is no simple verbal explanation for all of this. I believe that these stories are the best tools for relating the simple techniques that make attending the dying process a healing, spiritual experience.

A NATURAL PART OF LIFE

As you read these stories and my comments on them, I hope they convey the true essence of what happened. To give the stories balance, I have also interviewed some of the other people close to the dying person and included their comments.

I offer these stories and the way I experienced them in the hope that you may gain compassion and mastery over the process that we call death. It is important to explore the lasting effect that the death of a loved one has on the living. It is also important for our own peace of mind to remember the dying person's moments of joy, as well as their sadness at letting go of this lifetime. We can also remember that the joyous moments might not have been possible without honesty during these sad and painful times.

I have been privileged to help many people die over the last twenty years. What has been shared with me by my dying patients and their friends and family are the gifts of openness, authenticity, warmth, kindness and humor. These gifts continuously affect my own attitude about living.

Since my own two NDEs in 1975, I have had a strong desire to work with death and dying. My work with dying people ranges from medical research—six years at the University of Connecticut Medical School doing research on the aftereffects of an NDE—to independent work with dying people and their families. During workshops I have conducted for hospices, I have also heard numerous accounts of issues around dying. I have felt honored to witness and assist people in their transformation of suffering into honesty, compassion and release. For almost twelve years I led support groups for people who had NDEs— those people who have died but returned to their same bodies and lives. Also attending these meetings were caregivers, terminally ill people and others who sensed that death was an issue they needed to explore. I listened as they expressed their concerns about the issues of suffering and dying.

Death is a natural part of the web of life. Until the advent of hospitals we understood this fact of life and attended to our loved ones so they could die at home. Death was a natural part of our families and our communities. Now we can understand again that we can tolerate, comfort and transform suffering during the dying process. Most of the stories in this book demonstrate transformations from suffering to compassion, trust and love.

In almost every story, the dying person accepted his or her undeniable condition. And that acceptance transformed them. That transformation in turn became contagious among those of us who attended their dying process. Much of what we witnessed and participated in was nothing short of "little miracles." According to the definition in *A Course in Miracles*, a miracle is "the translation of denial into truth." This is exactly what we witness in the dying process.

Miracles occur naturally as expressions of love, and thus the real miracle is the love that inspires them. These miracles of love come quietly into our minds and hearts every time we touch our friends and loved ones as they—or we—are completing this life. We may touch physically, we may simply share our spiritual energy through intention, or our souls may meet in the briefest of instances.

Twice in my own NDEs, I stood outside of time looking from another dimension back into this one, and I reviewed my life of thirty-two years. I have never quite found the words to describe what it felt like when this intelligent energy/being held me as I relived all my relationships. What I learned in a nutshell is that love, supported by honesty, is what is important. The closest I can get to that experience again comes when I sit and attend someone in the dying process. The energy is there, with us and in us.

I offer you these stories in the hope that they will help make your journey of life and death easier. Read them slowly. Stop now and then, close your eyes, and just feel what comes into your heart. Again, *A Course in Miracles* says it best:

> *The miracle of life is ageless*
> *Born in time*
> *But nourished in eternity.*

ONE

Healing:
Barbara's Story

*M*y work with dying people probably would have never come about if I hadn't died myself. I know that sounds strange. How many of us die and get to come back and talk about it? Not many—we may think—but that's not true. In 1984, a Gallup poll reported that one in every nineteen Americans has had an NDE. And these first numbers include only adults. Since that time we have acquired data on childhood NDEs, and they are almost as prevalent as adult experiences.

I want to share my own NDE with you, most importantly to tell you about what we call the "life review." Our research shows that only in about 20 percent of NDEs is there a life review. Since my NDE over twenty years ago, I have focused my heart and my life on the knowledge I received from the life review.

Some NDErs report seeing their life review as if they are watching the pages in a book. Others describe it as a film. My life review appeared as a cloud filled with thousands of bubbles. In each bubble there was a scene from my life. I had the feeling I could bob from bubble to bubble, but overall it had the feeling of a linear sequence in which I relived all thirty-two years of my life.

During a life review, many of us experience not only our own feelings, but the feelings of everyone else—as though all other people participating in our lifetimes are joined. We can feel, then, how everything we've ever done or said affected others. The sense is that we don't end at our skin. It is an illusion that we are separate. This deep review of our life shows us that at a higher level of consciousness we are all connected.

This new perspective totally changes our values and attitudes about the way we want to live. Materialism decreases and altruistic values become greater in most NDErs' lives. Almost all of us talk about a sense of mission. If we were spiritual before, the shift in values and attitude is not as apparent as it is in someone like me. I had become an atheist when I numbed out at an early age. Subsequently, my changes have been obvious and profound.

A NEED FOR SURGERY

I was born with a deformity—a curvature in my lumbar spine called "scoliosis." It never bothered me until 1973 when it suddenly became the focus of my life. The pain emanating from my lower back became overwhelming, and the drugs I was given to control it numbed everything out. I was hospitalized four times in the next two years, each time for two weeks and with traction and injections of Demerol to help alleviate the pain. Looking back on it now, like many other NDErs I believe that my life had gotten off track and my back pain was a metaphor for my life.

In 1975, at the age of thirty-two, I was admitted for the fifth time to the hospital. I underwent surgery—a spinal fusion. I awoke after the five-and-a-half-hour operation in a Stryker-frame circle bed. This strange bed looks like a ferris wheel for one person. There are two big chrome hoops with a stretcher suspended in the middle. Three times a day the nurses would place three or four pillows over me and then another stretcher on top of them. They would strap these two stretchers together with me in the middle, like a human sandwich, and turn the bed on. It would rotate me up and then it would slowly move me around onto my belly. The pillows made it more tolerable because I was very thin. I had lost more than thirty pounds over the two years of pain and using Valium as a muscle relaxant. The surgery on my spine prevented me from any movement at all. I couldn't move. The bed moved me. The reason for using this bed, and for rotating me forward and face down, was to drain my lungs and allow the skin on my back to breathe so I wouldn't develop bedsores. I remained in this bed for almost a month, and then I was placed in a full body cast from my armpits to my knees.

About two days after surgery, complications set in and I started to die. I remember waking up in the circle bed and seeing this huge belly. I had swelled up. The swelling was pulling my incisions open and it hurt. I called for my nurse, and then I started screaming.

People in white came rushing in. It was a dramatic scene like you see on television. I had no idea what was going on because I hadn't become a respiratory therapist yet. It seemed like everybody was pushing carts and machinery, throwing things back and forth over me. They hooked me up to all kinds of machinery, tubes, monitors and bags.

FIRST NDE

Everything that was going on was loud and overwhelming. I lost consciousness.

I awoke in the hall in the middle of the night. The lights were dim. It was quiet. I looked up and down the hall and didn't see anyone. I remember thinking that if they caught me out of the circle bed I'd be in trouble, because I wasn't supposed to move. So I turned around to go back into my room and found myself looking directly into a public-address speaker. *This isn't possible,* I thought. I remembered seeing the speaker when I was admitted. It was mounted on the ceiling at least three or four feet above my head. I moved into my room and looked down into the circle bed and saw—me. I heard myself chuckle because "she" looked funny with white tape around "her" nose holding in a tube.

I was out of pain. I felt calm—incredibly peaceful—in a way I had never felt before. So I hung out with "her" for a while, but I knew that wasn't me.

Next, I was in total blackness. I don't know how I got there. I was floating in darkness with a gentle sense of movement. I knew I was moving away from this life. I had left this life behind.

Then I felt hands come around me and pull me into lush warmth. I realized it was my grandmother. I used to call her "Bubbie." She was pulling me close to her in a wonderful embrace. She had been dead for fourteen years, and I had never before thought of her existing beyond her death. But I knew I was with her.

I suddenly realized that what I had believed in the past might not be real. Maybe my belief systems were really messed up. Maybe this was real and everything else had been an illusion. As I was thinking about how off base my beliefs had been, and as I realized that my grandmother holding me was real, I felt like I released a load of toxic pain.*

---

* What I gave up was my old ineffective and even ignorant belief system,

And as I experienced that release, there was a sudden replay of every scene my grandmother and I had shared during our nineteen years together in this life. It wasn't just my memories of her—it was also her memories of me. And our memories became one. I could feel and see and sense exactly what she was feeling, seeing and sensing. And I knew she was getting the same thing from my memories. It was both of us together, replaying everything that we meant to each other. It was wonderful.

I can still replay each memory today, and they are as vivid as when they happened twenty-three years ago in my NDE. One of my favorite scenes is when we were cooking together. I was three or four years old. We were alone in her kitchen, but the whole family was going to come for dinner, so there was expectancy in the air. My Bubbie pulled over a heavy wooden chair from her kitchen table to the stove and picked me up and put me on it. She stood behind and very close to me to help and protect me. One at a time, she would put a little bit of mixture in my hand, and I would form it into a ball and drop it into this huge pot of boiling water. The pot was almost as tall as I was on the chair. The pungent smell of fish saturated the already humid air. I would put my hands to my nose and yell "Yuk!" And she would laugh. After we finished, she pulled the chair with me on it into the middle of the kitchen. I screamed and laughed because it felt like she was taking me on a ride. She wiped my hands with a wet cloth, but I smelled them and yelled "Yuk!" again. I watched her take a lemon and cut it in half. She rubbed a lemon half on my hands and then wiped them with her already stained and wet apron.

---

which *A Course in Miracles* calls the "ego," and which is also called the "false self" by Charles Whitfield and the self-psychologists. See the appendix for further explanation.

Then she looked at me with such love in her eyes and said, "Don't move. Bubbie will be right back." She came back with her hairbrush and brushed my hair for what seemed like a very long time. It felt so good. Then she made me long curls, twisting each lock of my hair around her fingers. When she was finished, and she lifted me down to the floor, I ran into her bedroom and looked in the mirror. I looked just like Shirley Temple.

When the whole family sat down for dinner that evening, she told everyone I had made the fish. My aunts looked at me, very impressed. And as they tasted it, they nodded their heads in approval and told my mother what a good cook I was.

After our memories ended, I stayed with my grandmother for a while. I loved her so much. Then I started moving away. I had no control over what was happening, but it felt all right that I was moving away from her. I understood that she would be waiting for me to return again, and that this place she was in was eternal. So was I. My life had been a brief moment in eternity, and I had no concerns or doubts that as this bigger eternal reality unfolded it was perfect. Besides, the one I had just endured for thirty-two years was so painful and constrictive. This new reality felt like it would continually expand and flow.

At that time I wouldn't have called where I was a tunnel, but later, as a researcher, I realized that "tunnel" is the closest word we have on this plane. Whatever it was that I was moving through started off totally black. Then I became aware that there was energy churning through the blackness. As I watched the energy move, shades of gray to almost white separated from the churning. Out of the darkness Light was coming, and the Light was moving way ahead of me. The Light and I were moving in the same direction, but it was far, far ahead.

My hands were expanding. They felt like they were becoming

infinitely large. A gentle breeze was wrapping around my body, and I could hear a low droning noise that beckoned me. This unusual sound was taking me to the Light.

Suddenly I was back in my body, back in the circle bed, and it was morning. Two nurses were opening my drapes. The sunlight was startling. It hurt my eyes. I asked them to close the drapes. I tried to tell my nurses and then several doctors that I had left the bed. They told me that it was impossible and that I had been hallucinating.

LIFE REVIEW

About a week later I again left my body in the circle bed. I had been taken off the critical list, but I was still dehilitated and sick. I had been rotated forward onto my face. I was uncomfortable. I seemed to have been left in that position for too long. I reached for the call button, but it had slipped away from where it was clipped on the bedsheet. I started to call, then yell, then scream frantically, but my door was closed. No one came. I wet the bed. I became hysterical. I separated from my body.

As I left my body, I again went out into the darkness, only this time I was awake and could see it happening. Looking down and off to the right, I saw myself in a bubble—in the circle bed—crying. Then I looked up and to the left, and I saw my one-year-old self in another bubble—face down in my crib—crying just as hard. I looked to the right and saw myself again in the circle bed, then to the left and saw myself as a baby—back and forth about three more times, then I let go. I decided I didn't want to be the thirty-two-year-old Barbara anymore; I'd go to the baby. As I moved away from my thirty-two-year-old body in the circle bed, I felt as though I released myself from this lifetime. As I did, I became aware of an energy that was wrapping itself around me and going through me, permeating me, holding up every molecule of my being.

It was not an old man with a long white beard. It took me a long time to use the word "God." In fact, I never used any word until I saw the movie *Star Wars* and heard about "The Force." By then, I was already reading quantum physics, trying to figure out how I could explain what had permeated me and was me . . . and you . . . and all of us. Now it was here, and it was holding me. It felt incredible. There are no words in English, or maybe in this reality, to explain the kind of love God emanates. God was totally accepting of everything we reviewed in my life. In every scene of my life review I could feel again what I had felt at various times in my life. And I could feel everything everyone else felt as a consequence of my actions. Some of it felt good and some of it felt awful. All of this translated into knowledge, and I learned—oh, how I learned! The information was flowing at an incredible breakneck speed that probably would have burned me up if it weren't for the extraordinary energy holding me. The information came in, and then love neutralized my judgments against myself. In other words, as we relived my life, God never judged me. God held me and kept me together. I received all information about every scene—my perceptions and feelings—and anyone else's perceptions and feelings who were in the scene. No matter how I judged myself in each interaction, being held by God was the bigger interaction. God interjected love into everything, every feeling, every bit of information about absolutely everything that went on, so that everything was all right. There was no good and no bad. There was only me and my loved ones from this life trying to be, or just trying to survive.

I realize now that without this God force holding me, I wouldn't have had the strength to experience what I am explaining to you.

I—we at this point, for we are one, a very sacred one—God and I were merging into one sacred person. We went to the baby I was seeing to my upper left in the darkness. Picture the baby being in a bubble and that bubble in the center of a cloud of thousands and thousands of bubbles. In each bubble was another scene in my life. As we moved toward the baby, it was as though we were bobbing through the bubbles. At the same time there was a linear sequence in which we relived thirty-two years of my life. I could hear myself saying, "No wonder, no wonder." I now believe my "no wonders" meant "No wonder you are the way you are now. Look what was done to you when you were a little girl."

My mother had been dependent on drugs, angry, and abusive, and my father wasn't there much of the time and did little to intervene. I saw all this childhood trauma again, in my life review, but I didn't see it in little bits and pieces, the way I had remembered it as an adult. I saw and experienced it just as I had lived it at the time it first happened. Not only was I me, I was also my mother. And my dad. And my brother. We were all one. Just as I had felt everything my grandmother had felt, I now felt my mother's pain and neglect from her childhood. She wasn't trying to be mean. She didn't know how to be loving or kind. She didn't know how to love. She didn't understand what life is really all about. And she was still angry from her own childhood, angry because they were poor and because her father had grand mal seizures almost every day until he died when she was eleven. And then she was angry because he left her.

Everything came flooding back, including my father's

helplessness at stopping the insanity. If my father was home when my mother exploded into one of her rages, he would close all the windows so the neighbors wouldn't hear, and then he would go outside and visit with them. Again I witnessed my brother's rage at my mother's abuse, and then his turning around and giving it to me. I saw how we were all connected in this "dance" that started with my mother. I saw how her physical body expressed her emotional pain. I watched as I grew up and left my parents' house when I was eighteen. By that point I had watched my mother undergo twenty-six operations, twenty-five of which were elective. I saw myself as a child praying for a doctor who could help my mother. One part of her body or another was always in pain. She had two spinal fusions on her neck, two or three on her lumbar spine. Both knees, both elbows and one wrist were operated on.

As my life review continued, I again experienced my mother starving herself because she was told she had gotten "chubby." Then she had to have several surgeries for intestinal problems and constipation, and during those stays in the hospital they would tube feed her because she was so thin. She even had her toes shortened. They called it "hammertoe" surgery. The real reason was because she had a huge collection of high-heeled shoes that were size four and one-half. (She always insisted on wearing spike heels even with her bad back.) Her feet were growing (as all of ours do as we get older) but she wanted them to remain a size four and one-half. I watched myself with her in a bubble as her orthopedic surgeon said, "Florence, you have two choices. Get shoes a half size bigger or shorten your toes!" He was laughing, but she chose the surgery. She was in plaster casts for six weeks, taking even more painkillers and sleeping pills.

I also saw her go through psychiatric hospitalizations. During one of these, around 1955, I couldn't visit her for three weeks. I was about eleven and was sure I had done something wrong. In one bubble I could see myself finally being allowed to visit her. I looked big for my age and my five-foot-two-inch frame towered over her four-foot-eleven one. She weighed about eighty-eight pounds. I was chunky. She lived on black coffee, sedatives, painkillers and tranquilizers. I loved to eat.

In the bubble I was pleading with her to cooperate with the doctors so she could come home. She said, "Oh, honey. This is like a job. I don't need to be in here, but Daddy has three (health insurance) policies so I make us money when I'm here. Blue Cross pays all the medical expenses, and we get to keep the rest from the other two policies." I could now feel her saying that and she meant it. She believed it. I continued watching and realized that nothing could have helped my mother because she had no real understanding about why she was there. I could hear myself saying, "No wonder, no wonder." And then the benevolent energy that was holding me would hold me tighter and with even more love.

We continued watching my mother in pain, always seeing doctors and always receiving prescription pain killers, sleeping pills and tranquilizers. My only feelings during this time were ones of loneliness. I felt so alone when she was in the hospital. Then I watched her abuse me when she was home. I could now feel that she abused me because she hated herself. I saw myself down on my knees by the side of my bed, praying for a doctor to help my mother. What I didn't realize as a child, but was understanding in the life review, was that she didn't want anyone to help her. She thought her job in life was to have doctors and be a patient. And she enjoyed being taken care of in the hospital.

I saw how I had given up "myself" in order to survive. I forgot that I was a child. I became my mother's mother. I suddenly knew that my mother had had the same thing happen to her in her childhood. She took care of her father during his seizures, and as a child she gave herself up to take care of him. As children, she and I both became anything and everything others needed. As my life review continued, I also saw my mother's soul, how painful her life was, how lost she was. And I saw my father, and how he put blinders on himself to avoid his grief over my mother's pain and to survive. In my life review I saw they were good people caught in helplessness. I saw their beauty, their humanity and their needs that had gone unattended to in their own childhoods. I loved them and understood them. We may have been trapped, but we were still souls connected in our dance of life by an energy source that had created us.

This is when I first realized that we don't end at our skin. We are all in this big churning mass of consciousness. We are each a part of this consciousness we call God. And we're not just human. We are Spirit. We were Spirit before we came into this lifetime. We are all struggling Spirits now, trying to get "being human" right. And when we leave here, we will be pure Spirit again.

As my life review continued, I got married and had my own children and saw that I was on the edge of repeating the cycle of abuse and trauma that I had experienced as a child. I was on prescription drugs. I was in the hospital. I was becoming like my mother. And at the same time, this energy holding me let me into its experience of all this. I felt God's memories of these scenes through God's eyes just as I had through my grandmother's eyes. I could sense God's divine intelligence and it was astonishing. God loves us and wants us to learn and wake up to our real selves—to what is important. I realized that God wants us to know that we only experience real pain if we die without living first. And the way to live is to give love to ourselves and to others. We are here to learn never to withhold our love. But only when we heal enough to be real can we understand and give love the way love was meant to be.

As my life unfolded before my eyes, I witnessed how severely I had treated myself because that was the behavior shown and taught to me as a child. I realized that the only big mistake I had made in my life of thirty-two years was that I had never learned to love myself.

And then I was back, but not in my body. I was behind the nurse's station. I saw a metal circle with pillows tossing behind glass. They were the pillows I had urinated on when I separated from my body. I was watching them in a dryer.

I heard two nurses talking about my case and about how my day nurse was so upset after she found me that they had sent her home early. Then they were saying that I was going to be in a body cast for six months, even though they had told me six weeks, because my doctors thought that I couldn't handle knowing. So they were not going to tell me the truth.

Then I was back in my body, back in the circle bed. The same two nurses came in to check on me and I said to them, "I left the bed again."

"No, honey. You're hallucinating," they said.

I was not on painkillers at this point, so I insisted, "No, I'm not hallucinating.* I left the bed."

---

* Hallucinations are usually experiences of seeing things or hearing voices that are really not there, in this reality. We will see something scary, for example, in the physical space we are in. By contrast, near-death and other transcendent experiences happen in other realities or dimensions. We may begin here, but the experience quickly moves to other realities.

"No, you're hallucinating. You can't leave the bed," they said.

"Please call my day nurse and tell her I'm okay," I responded. "Tell her I'm not angry with her. I know she was sent home early. And don't lie to me by telling me I'm going to be in a body cast for six weeks. Tell me the truth. I know I'm going to be in a body cast for six months. And you should have washed those pillows before you put them in the dryer. I don't care for myself, but I care for the next patient."

FOLLOWING MY HEART

A month after I came home from the hospital, my parents came over to visit me. They had taken care of my children for the month I was in the circle bed, so I understood why they couldn't visit me in the hospital. However, I couldn't understand why they weren't coming to my house. I spent every day in bed. I weighed eighty-three pounds and the body cast weighed thirty pounds. I wondered when they were coming so I could tell them about my experience. Finally they came, and I blurted out how much I loved them and that everything that had happened to us was all right. I think I even told them that I forgave them. They looked at me like I was really strange and quickly left. After that, I insisted on seeing a psychiatrist, hoping he would understand what I had experienced. The doctor I saw didn't understand. No one understood NDEs back then, so I realized that I couldn't talk about it. I spent the six months in the body cast, thinking about my NDE but not trying to tell anyone. Once I was out of the cast and went

---

Also, hallucinations are usually agitating and often transient in memory, whereas transcendent or near-death experiences are usually peaceful and benevolent, and we do not forget them.

through some physical therapy to regain my strength, I decided to put the NDE away and follow my heart.

First, I volunteered to work in the emergency room of the hospital where I had been a patient. I had many opportunities there to be with and touch dying people. I felt real when I worked there. And everyone else was real, too. In a setting where life and death are on the edge every moment, only truth is spoken. My personal life, however, was at the opposite end of the spectrum. My husband, my friends and most family members were caught up in their own games. No one seemed to be communicating honestly. There was so much denial of feelings. I can't deny that I too had been a part of it—part of the materialism and part of the numbness. But now I was different. It wasn't their fault. I had changed. The only place I felt real besides the hospital was on a college campus.

I became a respiratory therapist working in the emergency room and the ICU, and my patients were telling me about their experiences as they were dying. And the ones who returned to their bodies told me about their NDEs. I started writing about all this, in those days calling my topic "the emotional needs of critical-care patients." Surprisingly, I was being invited to speak at professional conferences and being published in respiratory therapy journals. The emotional needs of patients was a new and hot topic in healthcare in the late 1970s and early 1980s.

Finally, I became a researcher and could look for the answers I so longed to find. Because my research was conducted at a university medical school, all kinds of new knowledge were available to me. I could frame and reframe not only the hundreds of experiences I was studying, but also my own personal one. The story of my NDE is in this book so we can have a foundation for the way I participated in and describe the other stories you are about to read.

PROCESSING MY LIFE REVIEW

The NDE is never over if we invite it to continue to affect us. It can continue to grow in our lives if we nurture it. It continues to interpret for us what we are doing here, what life may be all about.

Before my NDE and life review, I knew I had been abused physically and emotionally by my mother and neglected by both parents. I remembered most everything. The problem was that those memories of abuse did not arouse any emotional reactions in me. In order to deal with the emotional and physical pain, I had numbed myself not only as a child going through pain, but also as an adult remembering it. I protected myself with my own "emotional Novocain," so I couldn't feel anything that had happened in my childhood. Unfortunately, the numbness continued in my adult life. Once I experienced my life review, I could remove the Novocain from my past and reglue the pieces of my life together. I could begin to learn about all the new feelings that were coming up.

Psychiatry calls emotional Novocain "psychic numbing." It is a common approach used by children to get through painful times. Once we grow up we have the choice of staying numb or remembering and working though all those buried but painful numbed-out memories. In my life review I also saw the beginnings of abuse in the way I was reacting to my children. For me it wasn't just a choice of numbness or healing. I needed to break the chain of abuse. I needed to save my children from what I had been through.

STARTING TO WAKE UP

I learned in my life review that the only thing that is real is love, and the only way to share love is by being real. Being real happens when we acknowledge our feelings and continually share our truth. When we feel our feelings and are real, we share our truth out of love. Then our relationship with God and our self is healthy.

My parents and the rest of my family and friends certainly weren't the exception to the rule when it came to not understanding my new attitude. I facilitated support groups for the International Association of Near-Death Studies (IANDS) for twelve years and the biggest problem NDErs talk about is that no one understands us. We experience a profound change in our values and attitudes and need to talk about it in a support group. It is as though we had lived our lives in black and white and were suddenly shown colors. We no longer fear death. And this is just the first of many paradoxes: Because we don't fear death, we don't fear living. We love life in a whole new way. We are more willing to take risks to help others. We work with the dying because we get as much as we give by helping.

Our research also shows that a history of childhood trauma, abuse and neglect is more frequent among NDErs than among the control group. Many people I have interviewed who have had an NDE came from an abusive childhood steeped in addiction. We all have the same story. We talk about how every time our parents started drinking or taking pills . . . they were gone. Even if their bodies were still there, they were gone. And so we grew up numb. Because our parents had numbed out, so did we. But our NDEs brought us back. They reminded us of who we are. And to maintain our real selves we have to learn to feel our feelings, share our truth and give our love. I wrote in detail about the childhood abuse factor in my last book, *Spiritual Awakenings*. Childhood abuse or trauma has always been of interest to me because of my own

history, and because I hear about it so often in support groups
or when I give talks. Now it has been demonstrated statisti-
cally in the research.*

I also wrote in *Spiritual Awakenings* that we should not
blame anyone, but instead we should break the chains of
abuse. When we die—if we reexperience our lives from everyone else's perspective as well as our own—there is only information and feelings, perceptions and knowledge. We really
can't judge or blame others because we suddenly understand
from where we and everyone else is coming. We only judge
here in this earthly reality. Over there, with God, I was just
learning about this. The knowledge of what had happened
was pouring into me, and I was saying my "no wonders!" over
and over again. I came to believe that God doesn't judge but
wants us to learn so we won't make the same mistakes again.
My experiences showed me that God wants us to extend love,
not fear. If I can understand my childhood, and I can name,
express and let go of the emotions I have held in since I was a
little girl, I won't repeat my past. My parents repeated their
pasts because they didn't know any better. Before my NDE
and my life review, the old way of conflict and numbness
controlled me. Suddenly, I was catapulted out of time and
embraced by a whole different way. Just as fast, I was back
here wanting to forge new ground. I have had a great opportunity and now I want to share it. But I don't blame, and I
certainly don't want to judge anyone, including my parents.

And now, almost twenty-three years later, my parents have
died—my dad in late 1992 and my mom in early 1994. My

---

* See K. Ring and C. Rosing, "The Omega Project," *The Journal of Near-
Death Studies* 8, no. 4 (1990): 211–239, and B. Whitfield, *Spiritual
Awakenings: Insights of the Near-Death Experience and Other Doorways to
Our Soul* (Deerfield Beach, Fla.: Health Communications, 1995).

life review had set the scene for the way I helped my father die and the way I observed my mother die. In fact, my life review, what I learned in it and, even more importantly, what I experienced in it—that a divine energy connects all of us—have since orchestrated all my relationships. With each person I have attended in the dying process, I have also witnessed this spiritual energy. I have given talks for hundreds of hospice workers, and almost everyone agrees that this energy is present. Hospice workers often tell me their stories of God's loving energy being present during a client's death.

In all of the stories in this book, I feel connected to this energy through my heart. The prayer within my heart is constant and is the background music orchestrating my experiences. When we are connected to God's loving energy, it is the most powerful force in the universe.

Two

Forgiveness: Sherry Rosen's Story

*S*herry Rosen made and canceled two appointments to see me in my office during the summer of 1995. She made another appointment in early September and then she had her husband call me and cancel it the day before. His voice over the phone sounded distressed, and I heard a lot of commotion in the background. I knew Sherry had cancer and that her chances of surviving were slim. I also knew she was young. I asked her husband if I could speak with Sherry, and she agreed to talk with me.

"It's too late. You can't help me now," Sherry said. "I don't want to be helped. I want to die."

"But I may be able to help make you more comfortable. If you feel you can't come to my office then I could come to your home. Would you like that?"

"Yes. Oh, yes," Sherry replied, and we made an appointment for the next day.

OUR FIRST VISIT

Driving to her home the next afternoon I felt some apprehension. It's always easier to see a new patient for the first time in my office. There we can talk one-on-one, even if family members come along. Going to someone's home can be more tense in the beginning; you never know what you'll find. I remembered the many shouting matches I had refereed in the past while doing home care for the dying. Often there is much anger in a family when one member is dying, especially within married couples. When someone is dying, someone else must stay behind, abandoned—no one takes care of either one's needs. Would I find anger in Sherry's house?

As I turned my car onto the side street near Sherry's house, I repeated my special prayer: "Dear God, Dear Spirit, please may I be an instrument of your healing energy, your love, your oneness and wisdom. Please help me to get out of the way, so you may come through." I had said this prayer hundreds, if not thousands of times since my NDE twenty years earlier. I hadn't read it anywhere; it just seemed to appear from my heart when I was about to help someone.

Sherry's home was in a beautiful townhouse community about twenty-five minutes from mine. A few people were standing around on the front porch. They smiled at me and told me to go in. More people milled around on the first floor. I introduced myself and expected to be taken upstairs. Instead, someone pointed me in the direction of a stairway that went downstairs. I walked down the steps, my logic telling me I was going to a basement, but instead discovered a downstairs bedroom suite complete with glass doors leading to a garden. There was also a fireplace and dressing area. It was beautiful, but still felt unusual, because the living area was above and we could hear people milling around above us.

Sherry was sitting up in a king-size bed. She was fair-skinned, with short, thick blond hair. I knew she was forty-eight years old, but she looked younger. And she didn't look sickly at all. Her weight seemed ideal, and she had big eyes and a beautiful smile. Sitting next to Sherry was her best friend and cousin, Lisa, and standing by the bed was Sherry's husband, Dave, who was tall and good-looking. Sherry and Dave made a stunning couple.

Sherry and Lisa were dressed as if they were about to go out. Each was wearing makeup and lots of jewelry. (Lisa told me later that Sherry had insisted that they look good for me.) Lisa and Dave both looked distressed as I sat down next to Sherry and across from them.

SHERRY'S CANCER

"Let's start from the beginning." I asked, "How did this start and how long ago?"

What I heard was a nine-month tale that was both tragic and romantic. As it unfolded I began to feel what they were feeling. I even sensed how easily Sherry was letting me in.

Sherry told her story in a raspy voice. "On New Year's Day I developed a cold. By the end of February it had dwindled down to a cough that was annoying and uncomfortable. Finally, on March 7th, I had an X ray and was then immediately sent for a CAT scan. The X ray had shown a small dot—just a shadow—on my left lung. After the CAT scan, the doctor showed us the report and it said "Cancer." A biopsy was done on March 13th and it confirmed the cancer. They told us it was extensive." Sherry started coughing, and in a strained whisper continued. "Now it's September, and I never realized it would grow as quickly as it has."

Dave took over, as Sherry dealt with her coughing by chewing on ice chips. "On March 12th," he said, "I was the old Dave. On March 13th everything changed, including me. Sherry and I went to the cancer specialist to discuss our treatment options. When we walked out of there, we both agreed that before the doctors did anything to her I would research everything I could."

Although she had trouble getting the words out, Sherry went on to say, "I looked inside myself, and I just knew chemotherapy wouldn't work. And it would ruin the time I had left."

Dave never took his eyes off Sherry. He continued speaking for her. "I'll never forget March 30. At 5:00 in the morning, Sherry woke up in a sweat and said she knew chemotherapy was not for her. That's when our life took the biggest shift. We weren't going to pursue traditional drug treatment for cancer. I realized that I couldn't go on working and still be there for Sherry, doing all the things I wanted to do with her. For one thing, I wanted to research alternative treatments for cancer. So I told three other insurance agents that I work with that I was turning all my business over to them. I cried and cried because I knew I was giving up fifteen years of work. But I also knew I had to be with Sherry."

And he was. Dave estimated that he spent eighteen hours a day or more learning about alternative care for cancer, including researching natural foods and networking with alternative cancer societies in California, Dallas and Denver. He learned about using herbs, enzymes, meditation, reflexology, massage, attitude change, video tapes and audio tapes—anything that might help manage the cancer.

"I took all this time off from work," Dave said. "We were doing well. We thought things were good. Sherry started feeling better, and we had hope. We were sure we were going to beat the odds, even though all the information that we were given indicated the worst. The nature of her cancer is large cell, metastasized and heavily established in her lymph nodes, abdomen and lungs. Another cancer doctor told us that we had six to nine months to live—I mean *she* had six to nine months to live. We thought for sure we were going to beat the odds.

"In the beginning of May, I was elated," Dave went on to say. "Sherry was doing better and I believed I could actually leave her and start working again. Then two weeks later her symptoms returned. Now I hated to even leave the house to go to the grocery store. With cancer there are two main fears: the fear of pain and the fear of being alone. I didn't want Sherry to have to worry about either of those fears. That's when we decided we would never leave each other's side, and we would do everything that we could to get Sherry the best care, no matter where it was or what it was. And we would make sure that she never felt pain. I know I can't promise her she will never feel pain, but I want to do everything in my power to make sure we've done everything."

Sherry had recovered from her coughing spell and continued their story. "We knew the cancer looked bad. Dave is in the insurance business and we had a terminal illness rider on our policies. So he was able to go to the insurance company and get the money that we needed now instead of after I'm gone. This way he didn't have to work, and we were able to do so many things that I have always wanted to do." She paused and smiled.

"I had to sign a form that said I had less than a year to live. That was the first time that the two of us had to face our reality on paper—and emotionally. Dave told me there wasn't time for me to deny all this. He said when I was ready I would sign, and he would always be there for me. I wanted to forget the paper I needed to sign. He didn't push me, but he had it all lined up when I finally decided to sign the paper. By then, my reports said I had six to nine months to live. I remember the moment I picked up the pen and signed. I was terrified, but somewhere in there I also felt a great release—like I was suddenly free."

"The first thing we did was go away to a place I had always wanted to see in Virginia, right at the base of the Shenandoah Valley. It's a bed-and-breakfast resort with three servants to every one guest. It was very expensive, but it was wonderful. We stayed there for four days." Sherry's smile came back. She was still for a moment, as though she was back there taking it all in.

Dave continued. "On June 23 we went to see a lung specialist. It was the second time we were seeing X rays. Up until this time we had never gone back to a doctor. We got through all the time between by talking—really talking—to each other and by sharing love. Even now we maintain our commitment to one another by never leaving each other's side. But the X ray taken on June 23 really shook us. It was shadowed with tumors. The number of tumors that had developed in three months was unbelievable. Each day since that June 23 X ray, I have watched another piece of Sherry's everyday activities taken away from her. But we have dealt with that."

GETTING READY TO DIE

Sherry picked up the next part of their story. "That's when I said to Dave, 'I'm getting ready to die. We need to go somewhere and be alone.' We called a travel agency right away, to go to Nantucket, because I love it there. But we couldn't get a room because the season had already started. So we made reservations on Cape Cod. We were going to be on a cove for eleven days, but they couldn't accommodate us until July 24.

We were scared I wouldn't make it, but for some reason . . .
Spirit let me go. Over time I got weaker, but my resolve got
stronger. Does that make sense?"

I had tears in my eyes, and I was staring right into Sherry's.
"Yes," I said. "That makes perfect sense."

Dave went on. "I was so worried about how I was going to
get you on the plane. You were so weak. I knew we were going
to have to use a wheelchair to get you to the plane, but I
didn't know how to tell you that. Then, while I was taking care
of checking us in, you just got right into that wheelchair. You
looked like a queen sitting there. You were bright and beautiful. I had been so nervous, thinking about how you were going
to take being put in a wheelchair, but you were terrific. The
skycap came and began pushing you along. I was walking
behind, trying not to cry. Suddenly you turned around in the
chair and said, 'Dave, I feel just like a queen!' And then you
said, 'Don't be so nervous. I'm being taken care of and this is
our vacation. Enjoy yourself!'"

Sherry finished the story. "I think everyone knew I could
die while I was there on the Cape. They all took such good
care of us and that gave us the opportunity to relax and enjoy
ourselves. We would have breakfast and dinner in the dining
room, and in between I stayed in our room because I was getting weaker. Sometimes I ate out on the balcony and enjoyed
the view.

"One night the water was so still that it looked like the boats
were sitting on a mirror. Dave ran off with his camera to cap-
ture the evening. The sky was without a cloud and jet black.
There was a quarter moon and millions of stars, all reflected in
the water. I sat on the balcony for so long that time seemed to
stop. I felt like I was looking into eternity. And I knew I was
safe and everything would be all right. I was ready for whatever

came. And you know what else? We joked and we laughed sometimes, too. We had a wonderful time."

Dave and Sherry looked at each other. They appeared to be joined in their memories. The four of us were quiet.

After a long pause, I asked Sherry how she was feeling now.

"I'm ready to die. I want to die now. People have been coming over, and I've been saying good-bye."

I nodded and said, "People who are really in touch with what is going on usually know when they are going to cross over. You are one of those people who is going through this with your eyes wide open."

Sherry nodded and said, "Every time I see someone now—that's it. I know I'm going to die soon, so I say my good-byes and don't want to see those people again. They are all in a lot of pain and I can feel their pain, so I want the good-byes over so I can stop feeling others' pain. And some of these people who were close to me—or thought they were close to me—hurt me. Maybe they hurt me long ago, but I can remember better now than I could before."

"So it's painful to have other people near you now." I needed to repeat what Sherry had said so I was sure I understood. She nodded yes and I then asked, "How are you feeling physically, now?"

"I'm jumpy," she answered. "It's hard to breathe. I'm scared. I ache. And, oh yeah! I'm very afraid of the pain getting too bad."

I smiled into Sherry's eyes. She certainly was in touch with herself, and that made my work easier. I addressed her fears. "I may be able to do some things that will help make you more comfortable right now. I can also show Lisa and Dave how to do these things so they can help you when I'm not here. Do you feel comfortable being touched, by me and by Dave and Lisa, too?"

"Oh, yes!" she whispered with enthusiasm.

HELPING SHERRY

I took off my rings and asked Dave and Lisa to do the same. I've done this hands-on work hundreds of times, and I've taught it to others. There's no wrong way to do it. All that is really needed is the *intention* to send love by touch.

"The main thing to keep in mind now," I told them, "is that for the next twenty minutes or so we are going to be sitting still. So it's important to find a comfortable position. Sherry, are you comfortable? Can I put pillows under your knees? Okay. Dave, is there a tape player in this room? Good. I brought some meditation music, or you can put on whatever music Sherry loves.

"The work that we are about to do is based on the idea that on a subtle level of reality, we are energy or we have energy flowing through us. The entire universe is made of this energy and we—all of us—can be instruments or conduits of an even greater energy simply by asking. That greater energy is healing and comforting, and through us, as its messengers, healing energy and comfort are passed to Sherry.

"Sherry is in physical pain and feels pain from other people. What we are about to do may help relieve her physical pain and even help to ease the emotional pain and anxiety that she has and is getting from other people."

I sat on the bed to Sherry's right and close to her. I was cross-legged. I had my right hand on her tummy, just below her navel, and my left hand was on her forehead. It helps to visualize or imagine that the energy flows out of the giver's right hand and then is taken in again by the left hand. The person leading the healing ceremony keeps his or her left hand higher up on the receiver's body than the right. This moves the energy flow up the receiver's body so the healing energy is moving in the direction of toe to head. Ideally, I would place my right hand on Sherry's tummy and my left over her heart, but she was having trouble breathing so I placed my left hand on her forehead instead.

Dave lightly placed both his hands on Sherry's feet. Lisa put one hand on Sherry's knee, the other on her hip. As the music played softly in the background, I asked if everyone was comfortable with me saying a prayer, and all three nodded in approval.

"Dear God," I said, "Dear Spirit, please make us instruments of your healing energy, your love, your oneness and your wisdom. Please help us to get out of the way so you may come through."

We closed our eyes, and for twenty minutes we sat together quietly. As the music played in the background, I visualized us surrounded in white light. Then I visualized the white light streaming through our hands and flowing into Sherry.

When we opened our eyes after twenty minutes, Sherry was relaxed and she looked peaceful. There was a softness and radiance in her face. I quietly said my closing prayer out loud: "Dear God, thank you for allowing us to be instruments of your love."

Sherry smiled and stretched. "Oh!" she said, "I didn't want to wake up. I feel relaxed and much better."

I looked at Dave and Lisa, who also appeared relaxed and at peace. "Do you two think you could do that again for Sherry without me? If you can do this—alone or together—three or more times a day, it will help Sherry and give her pain medication a boost."

"Oh, yes," they said together.

Lisa later told me, "I was confused by your presence, Barbara, not knowing why you were there. And I was apprehensive about the hands-on work because I was afraid I wouldn't be able to get it right. At the same time, I was willing to try anything to help Sherry. The hands-on work made a big difference in my being able to settle in and be with Sherry and the dying process in a relaxed way. As our first session with Sherry continued, I felt like you were there for me as well as for her. I also knew that Sherry was relieved by your presence. Then she knew for sure she wouldn't have to go to the hospital to die."

OUR NEXT VISIT

I came to see Sherry three days later, and the house was still humming with people. But no one went downstairs to see Sherry except Dave, Lisa and me.

When I walked into her room, Sherry was no longer in bed. She was sitting in a soft lounge chair with her feet up on an ottoman. The chair gave her better support than lying in bed on pillows, and Sherry stayed in that chair until she died. With Dave and Lisa standing close by, I sat on the floor in front of the ottoman facing Sherry and began massaging her feet.

When Dave and Lisa left to do something upstairs, Sherry confided in me, in a weak voice. "You've got to protect me. I can't stand the energy of everyone upstairs. I can feel their pain and it hurts me. I can't take any more pain. And I'm so angry with some of those people. I don't want to see them. I've said my good-byes and that's it." The entire time she spoke she was staring at her feet as I was massaging them.

"Whatever you want, Sherry. This is your process. You're running the show," I answered, continuing to lightly squeeze and rub her feet and legs to keep her in the present. "What else, Sherry? Come on. There's something else, isn't there?"

"Yeah!" Sherry's voice was weak and raspy with anger start-ing to pour out. "I'm mad at so many of them. I haven't talked to some of my relatives for years, and now that I'm sick, they're talking to me. There's a few I still won't talk to and they still keep coming over here."

"Your dad is remarried, isn't he? What happened to your mom?" I asked.

"I never knew my biological mother or my biological father," Sherry said with ice coming through her voice. "And my adop-tive mother died years ago. And when I was a child, sometimes I was treated poorly. My sister and I fought terribly. I was so hurt by everyone and I can't take their pain anymore!" Sherry drifted off somewhere. I continued to massage her feet.

After a few minutes I asked her, "Is that it, Sherry? Or is there anything else bothering you?"

She was quiet for a long moment.

"Look at this room," she answered with a pained look on her face. "It's awful. I usually never let it get like this."

"Like what?" I asked.

"There are bits of lint and stuff all over the carpet. Look over there."

I glanced over and grabbed some lint and little pieces of paper which were easy to see on the dark-colored carpet. Dave walked in. "What's the matter?" he asked, and looked at her.

"This room is a mess," Sherry replied. "The light is on in the closet, and the closet's a mess. Close the door, please, so I don't have to see it. And pick this place up. Make the bed. Dave, I always made the bed!"

Lisa walked in and understood what was going on now. She said in all innocence, "I'd do the laundry, but I don't know how to fold the towels and sheets!" Her voice trailed off with "Sherry has a special way."

"Well, I'll show you. I'm not dead yet, you know!" Sherry said and started to laugh. "Come on you guys. I'm not dead yet!"

Everyone, including me, got busy. We were all scurrying around and blowing off some steam. The three of them were throwing around a subtle level of insulting comments. Lisa came in with a load of clean towels.

"Okay, Missy. Which way is up!" and the two of them burst into laughter. And without missing a beat through her laughter, Sherry commanded Lisa to do it her way. Lisa complied, but made complaining comments the whole time. Lisa continued expressing herself as she ascended the stairway, and we could still hear her in the living room upstairs. Sherry was grinning.

"You know," I proclaimed, "this place does look better."

"Good. Now I can die," Sherry said.

Dave and Lisa came back into Sherry's room and they told me about their hands-on meditations over the last three days and how much they enjoyed doing them. And then we sat for twenty minutes with our hands on Sherry. Her breathing settled down and soon she sounded as though she was in a peaceful sleep. When we finished our meditation, I asked Sherry if she had felt or seen anything special during the hands-on work.

Sherry had a blank look on her face, and we leaned closer to hear what she was about to tell us.

"I saw mounds and mounds of shrimp," Sherry said.

Dave and Lisa turned to me. "What does that mean?" they demanded.

I paused, rubbing my chin for a while to increase the suspense. Then I proclaimed, "Sherry's hungry. It must be lunchtime."

We all laughed, and Dave and Lisa went upstairs to make some lunch for the three of them to share.

I wanted to spend some personal time chatting with Sherry, so I asked her who everyone was upstairs. I expected a running review as I often get from my clients—sometimes funny and sometimes sad—but instead, I saw Sherry shut down. She told me she was through with "all that" and didn't need to think any more about her life. She had always "held it in" and "tried to do the best" she could. Her life had been Dave and his work. She had worked with him and helped him every way she could. I respected her answer. I knew it was the best one she could give me.

As I said my good-byes I lightly chatted with the family members upstairs and told them I'd be back in a few days.

A SPIRITUAL EXPERIENCE

That evening, as I was starting to prepare dinner, the phone rang. "Barbara, it's David Rosen. This is it. Sherry's going, and she wants you here. How soon can you come?"

"It takes me about twenty-five minutes to get there," I answered. "I'll be able to leave in five minutes. Tell Sherry I'll be there in a half hour."

My mind was racing as I drove to Sherry's house. I prayed silently, trying to get myself centered and connected. To witness someone's dying is always a humbling experience, but I sensed somehow that this experience with Sherry was going to be particularly special.

Someone dying is so much bigger than any other ritual on this planet, except maybe childbirth. Souls come in. Souls go out. In most ways, death is beyond our comprehension. We live in a material reality that limits our ability to experience the sacred and celebratory side of death—the final passage from this physical reality to a nonmaterial and eternal reality.

This nonmaterial reality is spiritual, ineffable and a part of the divine mystery. It is the reality of God's world, not our earthly world, and sometimes we can only sense it through our hearts. As the Little Prince said, "It is only with the heart that one can see rightly. What is essential is invisible to the eye."

The enormity and elusiveness of this nonmaterial reality can perhaps only be understood in metaphor. As a respiratory therapist, I used large tanks of oxygen. Each tank contained enough compressed oxygen to make the pressure on the inner walls of the tank 2,200 pounds per square inch. That is an extraordinary amount of pressure. Yet we hooked the tank up to a patient who was receiving the oxygen in a slow steady stream. The oxygen at the patient's nostrils felt like a soft, gentle breeze because of a little device we use called a "reducing valve." Twenty-two hundred pounds per square inch went into the reducing valve, which brought the pressure down to a gentle stream going through the tubing that went to the patient.

As we take in reality, our brains work the same way as the reducing valve. Reality is huge. Its pressure is too big and too much for us to handle. Our brain, our reducing valve, allows reality to flow in a gentle stream so we can handle it without exploding ourselves. Helping someone die is as close as I can get, as close as any of us can get, to the huge reality beyond our individual ability to perceive. Ultimately all this is a mystery, but we can get closer to the mystery by allowing ourselves to experience death with openness, loss of ego and willingness to be aware of and open to our subtle experience.

Sherry was open to everything. I could feel it. I could almost see it. I had assisted in this ritual or rite of passage that we call "death" many times before. But this one was different. Sherry was different. I knew that all I had to do was get out of the way. She was open, and Spirit would do the rest.

I parked and went in. I descended the stairs to one of the most remarkable nights I have ever witnessed and participated in. It was both subtle and blatant.

Sherry was still sitting in the chair, with her feet up on the ottoman. Her breathing was labored and loud. It sounded like a moan from deep within her chest. Her shoulders flew up with every inhalation, and her head was tilted to one side, almost touching her shoulder. I sat down next to her and gently moved her head back so that it was resting on a pillow. I took her pulse: it was racing. Dave hovered nearby with a look of bewilderment and helplessness, his eyes huge.

"Is this it?" he asked. "She's not in pain, is she? Will it be over soon?"

"It could be over soon," I answered, "and then again she could rally. We never know for sure until it's over."

Dave sat down next to Sherry. One of the soft music tapes I had brought was playing in the background. The lights were low. We both just sat there, wide-eyed and absorbed in Sherry.

This is the midwife role. We are just there, witnesses to the dying. We are also there to assist the dying in whatever they need or desire—physically, emotionally and spiritually. We are their advocates and their validators. Most of the time, though, we just sit and are with whatever is happening.

Dave began to quietly read from Sherry's copy of *A Course in Miracles*, one of her favorite books. I studied this room we were in. Around the fireplace were hand-drawn pictures, obviously done by little children. Although Sherry and Dave had never had children of their own, there were small children in their lives—two were nieces and one was a child of a friend. The pictures were signed "I love you, Sherry" and "I miss you, Sher." Love poured out of the children's art, right into this radiant forty-eight-year-old blond woman who was now straining to take each breath.

About a half hour into our sitting, Sherry opened her eyes. "Why haven't I died?" she asked. "You promised me I wouldn't suffer and I'm in pain. Why haven't I died?"

I looked closer into Sherry's face. "I don't know why you haven't died. I thought you were going to. It looked that way. But we can't control when. That's in God's hands. Are you suf-fering? Tell me what you are feeling. I'm here for you, and I'm going to stay just as long as you want me to, or until you die. Whichever happens, I'm here with you."

"Oh, God, I just hurt," Sherry answered. "I can't explain it. I just need to be rid of this body."

"Dave," I asked, "when was her last dose of morphine? Let's call the doctor and see if we can up her dose, or split it and give it to her more often."

As I turned back to Sherry, she had a full, beautiful smile on her face. Her skin was smooth and waxen-like, with light coming through it. "Why, you look radiant!" I told her. She laughed and said, "I feel good, if it weren't for this pain." I assured her that we were going to do our best to keep her out of pain. And we did.

The doctor quickly agreed to increase Sherry's dose of mor-phine. And while we waited for the extra dose to work, I helped Sherry to freshen up. I brought a toothbrush and basin to her, and she brushed her teeth. Then I sponge-bathed her and massaged her feet. During this twenty-four-hour vigil, Sherry never wanted to eat or drink and only ingested ice chips. We helped her to the bathroom just once.

Lisa came down to join Dave and me in our vigil with Sherry. She brought two candles, and we sat together in the dimly lit room, witnesses to Sherry's dying. Lisa told us stories of her childhood with Sherry. Dave reminisced about dating Sherry. He brought out pictures of the two of them. We took turns massaging Sherry's feet, and we did hands-on prayer and meditation. Sherry looked at us with such love in her eyes. As the night wore on, she seemed to become more spirit and less physical. I asked Lisa and Dave if they could see this happening, too. They both saw it. Sherry smiled and said, "That's what it is. I feel so different. Oh, Dave! Please read to us from *A Course in Miracles.*"

As he read, I studied Lisa and Dave's faces. They were flushed. I felt my face and it was hot. The candlelit room took on a golden hue.

Around midnight or a little later, Lisa kissed Sherry good night and went upstairs to sleep on the living room sofa. I heard Sherry's parents and other family members leave. Sherry's sister, Nina, stayed and slept on the den sofa, but she never came downstairs. The few times I went upstairs during the night, however, I would find Nina awake and crying. Only Dave, Lisa or I ever went downstairs.

As the night wore on, Dave and I settled down together, on the floor facing Sherry, with our backs against a huge chest of drawers. A candle burned above our heads, on the chest, and another candle burned next to Sherry on her bedside table. She was in a deep sleep and began the labored breathing again. The music played continuously in the background, the tape player automatically playing the other side of the cassette. Dave and I began breathing with Sherry and each breath seemed like it could be the last. Sherry's face was outlined by the candlelight, and another, other-worldly light seemed to be streaming from her face. Spirit was infusing the room, and we could feel it.

At one point, a piece of wax from the candle above fell down between Dave and me. He picked it up, and we both looked at it in awe. It was shaped like an angel, wings and all. We knew then that we were in some kind of altered state.

Around 3:00 A.M., Dave and I agreed to take one-hour shifts watching Sherry while the other one slept. Dave was going to sleep first, but before he did, he said, "Barbara, it seems like everything has changed here, in this room. It's like we're suspended in another kind of reality. What is this?"

I was quiet for a moment and then answered him. "Sherry is almost spirit now. And that spirit is surrounding us. She is slowly making her transformation from physical energy to spiritual energy and we are sharing that journey with her."

""It's amazing," Dave said, almost laughing as he settled down to sleep for an hour.

We took turns sitting and sleeping all night. At 7:00, Sherry opened her eyes and said, "Oh, God. Why am I still here?" But before I could answer, she continued, "I know. This is a dress rehearsal."

"That sounds good to me," I answered. "But, Sherry, is there something else, something holding you back? We're alone. You can tell me if something else is going on."

"I want to get out of here," she said. "I need to get rid of this body. I'm ready and I thought I could just release myself and go. But it's not happening."

"Where do you think you are going to go?" I asked.

"Well, I don't think it's heaven like I thought of heaven when I was a little girl." Her whisper trailed off, and I thought I saw a flash of fear.

Then a look of real fear came over her face.

"Sherry, what's scaring you?" I asked, alarmed.

"There are some people who were cruel to me as a child," she answered. "I remember the pain."

I waited for her to go on, but suddenly she had a coughing spell that lasted for several minutes. She was drenched in perspiration. I took a damp cloth and freshened her face and neck. She couldn't go on speaking, and I didn't push her. Dave brought me some coffee, and we decided I should go home and take a few hours for myself. I promised I would be back about noon.

It was startling to walk out into the sunshine. A big part of me didn't want to leave Sherry, but I needed a shower and to lie down in my own bed for an hour or so. I had this strange feeling that I had "shrunk" internally to make "room" for Sherry. I told that to my husband, Charlie, when I came in. "It seems like I've become a part of Sherry's transformation to spirit." Charlie understood it all, and he told me I needed a warm bath and some rest for a few hours. Later, I told him about Sherry's fears. "She told me about some cruel people who hurt her in her childhood and who have been dead for some time. Do you think somewhere in the back of her mind Sherry's afraid to die because she thinks these people might be waiting for her?"

Charlie pondered the question for a few seconds. "That could be it. It's worth bringing it up again with her and reassuring her that she doesn't have to deal with those people if she doesn't want to." I knew deep in my heart he was right. I knew I would find the right moment to reassure her.

I pulled up to Sherry and Dave's house at exactly noon and saw Nina and Lisa sitting on the front steps. Nina was crying. "What's up?" I asked.

Nina and Lisa told me that Sherry's parents were in synagogue praying for Sherry to die. Lisa's parents were there, too. The parents had been told not to come back to the house afterward, and it was tearing them apart. They had asked to come back and had promised to stay in the living room to pray. They would not go downstairs. They wanted to hold a prayer service for Sherry in the house. They would respect her need for privacy, but they wanted to be in the house. Nina and Lisa didn't know what to do.

"Well, I'll go in and see how Sherry is," I said, "and try to talk to her about it."

When I walked into Sherry's room, the first words out of her mouth were, "Barbara, I love you. It is so wonderful that you are here. You understand. You're the only one. I wish we would have met earlier."

"I agree, Sherry. Next lifetime, let's make sure we meet when we're kids and grow real old together." We both smiled at the thought. "But now I have to discuss some heavy stuff with you. Are you up to it?"

"What is it?" she asked with a hint of disgust.

"I understand that having people in the room is painful for you."

"Everyone makes me hurt except you and Dave and Lisa," she said.

"Okay, so we'll keep everyone out of the room. But what about a prayer service in the living room right over our heads? Your parents and your aunt and uncle have been in synagogue all morning, and they've said prayers for your release. They want to come here this afternoon and do it again. I think it would be wonderful to feel the energy of a prayer service pouring down from above us, and we can even open the door to the stairs and hear some of it. They need to be here, Sherry, but they don't have to come downstairs if you don't want them to. How about it?"

Sherry looked at me with love in her eyes. "All right. But I need my medicine," she said. I gave her her next dose of morphine and then kissed her on the forehead. "I'll be right back. I need to make the arrangements for the prayer service dedicated to Sherry Rosen." We both smiled.

When I told Lisa and Nina they were relieved, and they called the whole family to come over.

People started coming to the house about an hour later. Over our heads, we heard the preparation for the prayer service. Dave came downstairs for a few moments and asked Sherry if she wanted him to stay with her or go upstairs and pray. "Go upstairs and be with them," Sherry said and smiled at him. "Barbara and I are all right." She had been holding my hand and she squeezed it and said, "Dave, go ahead and ask Barbara. I haven't asked her. I've been waiting for you." Dave looked toward me and said, "Barbara, Sherry and I would like you to officiate or speak at her memorial service." And he swung around and headed for the door.

Sherry said, "I know what we are doing is unusual. My family was very upset for a long time about my wanting to die at home. They think I should be in a hospital. I don't want to be in a hospital. I want to be here, and you have made that possible. And I don't want a regular funeral. I want a memorial service where anyone who wants to can get up and talk about me when I was alive. I want it to be a celebration of life. Then I want everyone to enjoy a beautiful dinner. And then I want to be cremated, not buried. My family is having the worst time with this last part. I know it."

"Sherry, don't worry," I answered. "You'll get exactly what you want." Saying that, I remembered Sherry's fears of some people from her past. "Sherry, are you thinking much about those people who were cruel to you?"

"Yes, I can't get them out of my mind. One of my nieces asked me to kiss and hug them for her when I see them. I don't want to get near them. I can't forgive them for what they did to me when I was little and couldn't defend myself against their abuse."

Anyone dying—whether they are on pain medication or not—may be perceiving their reality through a fog. Remembering that Sherry was on morphine, I moved in closely to have total eye contact with her. I was no more than three inches away from her face. I reassured her by saying, "You do not have to see or forgive anyone over there for a long time, or never. It is your choice. There's no cruelty or abuse with God on the other side."

She sat staring into thin air for a while. Then she said, "Maybe they are already back here and are babies." We both giggled. Sherry then announced in a strong voice, "I want to come back as David Letterman's baby!" And we both really laughed.

THE PRAYER SERVICE

As the men upstairs began chanting in Hebrew, Sherry slumped back farther into her chair and became ashen gray. I sat next to her and said, "Dave hasn't been downstairs with us for a long time."

"Yeah, we haven't seen Lisa either," Sherry answered in a weak and raspy voice. "Lisa's with her dad and mom. She must have really wanted this prayer service here. She's hurting badly, I know."

I picked up her hand and held it near my face so she would look at me. "Tell Lisa that," I said. "If you forget, can I remind you when she's back in here?"

"Yeah. You can do anything you want, Barbara. I trust you," Sherry whispered. With that as permission, I got up and went to the double doors to the stairwell. I opened them wide for the first time.

"Well," I declared, "let's allow all of the prayer service to flow in here. We, and this room, could use it."

The chanting continued and grew in power. I had not been in a synagogue in years, and I listened intently to the beautiful sounds of people chanting and singing in Hebrew. Their voices took me back to what seemed like another lifetime of memories.

Then Sherry said, in a voice that was becoming increasingly weak, "They better be praying for me to die."

A half hour or more into the chanting, we suddenly heard a single male voice, clear, beautiful and quivering. "How do I love thee? Let me count the ways." Sherry's father was standing in the hall, at the top of the stairs, reciting Elizabeth Barrett Browning's poem.

> *I love thee to the depth and breadth and height*
> *My soul can reach, when feeling out of sight*
> *For the ends of Being and ideal Grace.*
> *I love thee to the level of every day's*
> *Most quiet need, by sun and candlelight.*
> *I love thee freely, as men strive for Right;*
> *I love thee purely, as they turn from Praise.*
> *I love thee with the passion put to use*
> *In my old griefs, and with my childhood's faith.*
> *I love thee with a love I seemed to lose*
> *With my lost saints,—I love thee with the breath,*
> *Smiles, tears, of all my life!—and, if God choose,*
> *I shall but love thee better after death.*

I was deeply moved hearing Sherry's father talking to his dying daughter through the words "How do I love thee?" I turned my face away from Sherry and released a deep, but quiet, sob. Tears streamed down my face. I tried to control them, but to no avail.

"Why are you crying, Barbara? What's wrong?" Sherry asked. There was so little strength in her voice that I thought she could be dying.

"Oh, I'm sorry," I answered. "I got carried away by my own grief. My father died three years ago and hearing your dad say that beautiful poem to you really got to me. I just miss my dad so much."

We were silent for less than a second and Sherry suddenly moaned and began to choke. She whispered, "Their prayers must be working. I must be dying. I feel awful."

This is it, I thought. *Their prayers are releasing her to die.* Then suddenly Sherry began to vomit. I grabbed the trash basket and held it under her face, one hand on the basket and the other holding the weight of her head "It's all right, Sherry," I said. "It's all right."

Sherry finally stopped and put her head back on the pillow. She smiled weakly at me. "I thought I was dying."

"So did I," I answered as I gently wiped her face with a moist washcloth.

"But, Barbara, now I feel better. Oh, no. I wanted to die and I feel better."

"Wait a minute," I countered. "You feel better? Was there pressure in your abdomen that's now relieved?"

"Yes," she answered. "How did you know that? There is so much going on in my body that I couldn't tell that from all the other pain until now because it's gone. What does that mean?"

"It means that whatever you're taking by mouth is probably not getting through your digestive system. We know your lungs are blocked, but we didn't realize your digestive tract is blocked, too, and only some of the morphine but not all of it is getting through. It means you'll have your wish to die, soon. But we need to change how we've been administering your pain medication. From what I just saw, you probably threw up a great deal of the morphine. It's just not being absorbed. We need to call the hospice or your doctor and get your pain medication prescribed in a different form."

I called up to Dave and explained what had just happened. He put in a call to the hospice. Then I went upstairs and told the large group of family and friends what had just happened. They had a lot of questions, and I tried to answer them as honestly as I could.

"Oh, my goodness," Sherry's father said, showing his anguish. "We prayed for her to die, and now she is in even more pain."

"No," I answered him, "she's not in more pain. Her pain has been relieved. She's more comfortable now. Your prayers worked. It's God's will when she dies, but your prayers have made her more comfortable and have helped her to feel more peaceful. And your reading of the poem was wonderful. Thank you."

At that moment, I believed in my heart and still do that something eternally powerful came through the prayer service. As I heard myself answer Sherry's father and as all this settled in, I realized Sherry had gotten what she needed—not what we thought she needed. From the prayer service on, there was a subtle but noticeable shift that we can only call "grace."

The hospice put us through to a physician on call and he and I discussed alternative medications. He prescribed Duragesic fentanyl in patch form. Dave went to get it. Sherry held my hand tightly until he came back. I placed a patch on her hip. We waited for it to work. Soon she smiled and relaxed. "Dave," she said "go tell everyone I feel better. And stay up there and eat some lunch."

I sponge-bathed Sherry and helped her change into a soft

pink nightgown. "Would you like me to draw the drapes so you can rest now that you're more comfortable?" I asked.

"No. Why don't you turn on the TV? I haven't watched it in a long time," she answered. I was surprised and I smiled at the thought of watching television at a time like this, but I went to the set and turned it on.

As the picture came on I recognized a scene from the film *Steel Magnolias* It was the scene where Sally Field, as the mother, is sitting by her daughter's bedside in ICU. Her daughter, played by Julia Roberts, is in a deep coma and dies. I turned quickly to Sherry and said, "I'll change it!"

"No," said Sherry. "Leave it on."

"Have you seen this?" I asked with deep concern.

"Yes. It's okay. I want to see it again. Come here and hold my hand."

I sat next to her and together we watched the next scene, at the cemetery immediately after the daughter's funeral. Sally Field gives a powerful performance as a parent in the first raw stages of grief. The characters played by Shirley MacLaine, Dolly Parton, Olympia Dukakis and Daryl Hannah surround her with concern and love, but they do not try to take her pain away. They are "midwives" to her pain, witnesses to the experience. But they never intervene in her pain. My heart was aching with them as the scene ended.

This scene, and my work with Sherry, reminded me of what Charlie had said about a guideline a hospice pioneer had told him more than twenty years ago: Reverse the old adage of, "Don't just stand there, do something!" into "Don't just do something, stand there!" These are often wise words for those who assist people as they die. We don't necessarily know what the dying person needs. Sometimes they don't know either. Other than caring for their physical needs, I have found that the best plan is no plan. When I feel something has to be done, I pray. I never pray out loud unless I know the dying person is comfortable with that, and if so, sometimes we pray together. And then we can trust that Spirit will provide whatever is needed.

Suddenly Sherry interrupted my thoughts. "All right," she said. "I've had enough. Let's see what else is on." I channel-surfed but there was nothing interesting. "What do you have on tape?" I asked, and bent over to look at them stacked on the VCR.

"Please put on the one marked 'Sherry and Nina's childhood,'" she answered.

"Okay, this is the beginning of your life review," I told her. I found the tape, inserted it in the VCR and sat down next to Sherry, taking her hand.

"What do you mean?" Sherry asked.

So I told her about my life review and about how some NDErs have experienced the same thing. I told her about us reliving our lives from a higher perspective, with Spirit or God holding us and helping us through.

For the next forty-five minutes, we reviewed her childhood, watching and never saying a word. We saw every birthday party she and Nina had had from the age of one to twelve. There were many trips as well, to Florida and Niagara Falls.

Sherry asked, "Well, what do you think?"

"It's more important what you think, Sherry," I answered. "What did you see?"

"I saw a lot of love, but I don't remember it that way." She was almost whispering.

"Well, maybe something was getting in your way back then. At least that's the way it was for me. When one person abuses us when we are little, it may be harder to feel the love of the others," I answered.

"Oh!" Sherry said slowly and thoughtfully.

"But what do you see, Barbara? Please tell me." Sherry was almost begging now.

"I see many sunny trips to Florida. I see that they took you along. They didn't leave you with a sitter. I see birthday parties, celebrations where you are the center of attention. I believe I see love. Do you?"

"Yes, I do." Sherry remained quiet for a long while. She held my hand tightly the whole time.

Finally, she broke the silence. There was tenderness in her voice. "Barbara, I think I'm all right now. You look tired. If you want to go home, go ahead. If I start to die, Dave will call you right away."

"Okay, Sherry. I'll come Monday for a regular visit. That's the day after tomorrow. It will be time to change your patch and I'll do it." I kissed her, and she once more told me she loved me. I looked deeply into her eyes and had no doubt that she did. I also saw a strength there that she didn't have earlier. Sherry was back. I wondered how many more days she could go on like this.

THE NEXT DAY

The next day, Sunday, Dave phoned me at exactly 3:00 P.M. "Barbara, I don't know—she could be almost dead," Dave said, "but she's still breathing like she did with us. I don't know what to do. We're all sitting here just watching her."

"You and Lisa?" I asked.

Dave answered, "Oh, everyone is down here. Sherry's father and mother, Aunt Judy and Uncle Bill, Nina and Harold, Nina's son Stephen." He went on to mention several other names that I did not know.

"Dave, when did all this happen?" I asked. "When did everyone come downstairs to be with Sherry?"

"Right after you left yesterday. Oh, Barbara, it's been beautiful. This family is really something. It's like it was when it was just you, Lisa and me with Sherry but now the whole family is part of it, too. This family is healing. Barbara, I think Sherry is dying now. What should I look for?"

"Are her eyes open?" I asked. "Are they gray, like they've lost color?" After I said that, I realized I should stop asking him questions and just go over there. I said, "Dave, tell you what. I'll leave in about five minutes and I'll be there in a half hour."

When I arrived and walked downstairs, the effect was astounding. There were people on chairs lined up three-quarters of the way around the room. But my focus was on Sherry. I pulled up a chair next to her and opened one eye and then the other. They were gray. Dave handed me a flashlight and I checked her eyes again. Her pupils were fixed. Her breathing was loud and infrequent. She was drooling. I took a tissue and wiped her mouth and chin. I slowly moved her head back to the pillow behind her so the drooling would stop. I closed both of her eyes gently. "Oh, thank you," Sherry's Aunt Judy said. "She's been like that for quite a while and I didn't know what to do."

"I know," I said. "She will go on like this for a while and then her breathing will just stop. Right now she may still be here, although I think perhaps she's not in her body and she's not suffering at all." I made sure I was having eye contact with everyone as I looked around the room. Everyone was calm. The mood was less about grieving and more about waiting. There were some tears over the next hour and a half, until Sherry took her last breath, but not as much as would be expected. Everyone understood that they were part of the process of waiting.

Lisa knelt on the floor in front of me and next to Sherry. I was rubbing Sherry's arm the whole time. Lisa, totally wide-eyed, said, "We all sat in here last night—my parents and everyone—and, Barbara, it was wonderful. After that, I fell asleep on the living room sofa and Dave woke me up at 5:00 this morning. We both watched Sherry breathe for a half hour. We thought that was going to be it. But then Sherry woke up. Dave went to take a shower, and I helped Sherry to the sink and she washed up. My parents and everyone have been here all day and we've read prayers. Sherry couldn't read her prayer anymore, so I read it for her.

"We thought she had gone early this afternoon," Lisa continued. "She stopped breathing for a little while, and we were all here staring at her. At 2:30, she opened her eyes and said, 'What? Did you all think I was going to die? It was only a dress rehearsal!'"

Dave moved in close and said, "She asked me to hug her, and when I did, she put her arms around me and held me, too. She had such strength in that hug. I don't know where she got it from. Then she said in my ear, 'You've been the love of my life.'"

"Barbara," Lisa said with sorrow and exhaustion in her voice, "I need to go upstairs now. I need to lie down for a few minutes."

"Go, Lisa," I answered her. "It's all right."

Lisa's mother, Aunt Judy, was sitting on my other side. She said, "After Sherry hugged Dave, I told her it was all right to go. Sherry said good-bye to me and to Bill, and to everyone in this room. One at a time she told us she loved us and we told her we loved her back." And she put her head down and her hand over her eyes and sobbed.

Suddenly, Sherry made a loud gasp and stopped breathing.

She started breathing again about thirty seconds later, but her breaths became further and further apart after that.

Aunt Judy, with tears occasionally running down her cheeks, began to reminisce. "I remember the first time I laid eyes on Sherry. My sister said to me, 'Come on and see this baby with me. I requested a boy baby, and they just called me that they have a girl baby.' We went to a foster home and there was Sherry, about a week old, lying in this crib. She was so beautiful. I said to my sister, 'You're going to leave her?' So she took her. I had Lisa a short time later. Sherry and Lisa were best friends before they could talk."

Someone else said, "We couldn't understand when Sherry wouldn't go to the hospital. We'd never seen anyone do this at home. We were so apprehensive about it, but now that it's happening—it's all right."

I smiled and said, "This is the way dying used to be. We always surrounded and comforted our dying loved ones at home."

Sherry's breathing had stopped again for what seemed like much longer. I focused on her. We all focused on her. Her skin was radiant and translucent. She was peaceful. Everyone in the room was peaceful. This was it. Sherry had finally died.

AFTERWARD

The peacefulness kept us glued to our seats for another twenty minutes or so. After all the gut-wrenching waiting, a stillness had enveloped us all. No one wanted to or could move.

Finally, I asked Dave to call the hospice. It would send out the nurse assigned to her case in an hour or so. Because Sherry had requested cremation, I realized that she would not be taken to a funeral home and then be prepared to be "viewed" again by family and friends. This was the last time her family would see her.

Jewish law doesn't really allow for cremation, and Sherry's family was uncomfortable about what was going to happen to her body. I had suggested to Dave and Lisa that the three of us prepare Sherry's body and then ask the family back into her room to see her. I told everyone what the three of us were going to do, and that our preparation—the bathing of her body and changing of her clothes was a ritual as old as Judaism. I asked them to give us an hour. Everyone filed out quietly and tearfully.

I grabbed Nina and said, "Nina, you're Sherry's sister, and you belong in this ritual, if you'd like to be here. We could certainly use your help moving her. If it's too much for you, you can just sit back while we do the rest. In fact," I said to Dave and Lisa, now that it was just us, "if this is too much for any of you, just move back and sit down, or if you have to, leave the room."

Nina stayed and the four of us began to prepare Sherry for her loved ones' final visit with her. We slid our hands under her body, and we gently lifted her from the chair onto her bed. We put pillows behind her back so she was sitting up. We got washcloths and a basin filled with warm water. Following in the Jewish tradition, we prepared her body by very gently giving her a sponge bath. Occasionally, I would talk to Sherry, telling her that if she was still in the room, everything was all right. I told her we were going to do everything she had requested for her memorial service.

Lisa shared with us her last conversation with Sherry. "Sherry told me this morning about when she threw up during the prayer service. She said that while it was happening, she was thinking she wanted to tell me, 'I know this is hard for you, Lisa. I know it's hard for you to see me like this, but it's not hurting me.' Sherry was always concerned about how I felt," Lisa concluded.

Nina was crying. "I wish we could have been closer." She tenderly helped dry Sherry, then we put a beautiful nightgown on her. Lisa put Sherry's lipstick and eye makeup on. Then as she brushed some color on Sherry's cheeks, she said, "I always used to do this for her. We played this way when we were kids. And even until the end she would ask me to put makeup on for her." Then Lisa fixed Sherry's hair.

I turned to Nina. "Nina, are the flowers upstairs still fresh?" She went upstairs to retrieve them, and I prayed silently that this wasn't too much for her. She was such a kind soul. Nina returned with one vase after another of beautiful flowers that we placed around the room.

Dave said, "Let's dim the lights."

In the darkened room, we stepped back and looked at Sherry's body and all around the room. We realized we had transformed the room and the mood into a special place for "one last beautiful visit." Finally, we put Sherry's favorite stuffed animal in her arms.

I had prayed silently throughout this ancient ritual of preparing the body. I looked into the faces of Nina, Dave and Lisa. They were all right. I said a prayer of thanks—again silently. Then we called everyone back.

They filed in quietly. Aunt Judy was the first to speak. "Oh! She looks so peaceful. I can't believe she isn't still around. This is all so new, and Sherry was only forty-eight."

"I can't believe it either," Sherry's father said as he wiped away his tears. Then everyone talked together softly for an hour. They shared memories, and they shared their disbelief and bewilderment over how young Sherry was and the way she had handled her illness and her death.

Lisa spoke to everyone in the room. "As soon as Sherry learned she had terminal cancer, she knew this was the way she wanted to die. Everyone was giving her advice, but she stood her ground, and you let it happen. You let her have her way. She would have died anyway, but this way Sherry died happy. And she had some fun to the very end. Right, Sher?" And she looked at Sherry's body.

Dave reminisced, too. "Sherry taught me so much. I remember when we started living together she gave me an ultimatum. 'You either pick up your own clothes or I'm out of here.'" And he smiled as he stared at her and cried.

Someone else said, "I've gone along with everything Sherry wanted since her illness began, but I don't know if I can handle this cremation business."

Dave answered, "That is what Sherry wanted. We can't deny her that. As soon as the hospice nurse is through here, the people from the crematorium are coming. And then as soon as I can arrange it, we are going to have a memorial service for Sherry at the community center. After that we will have a big catered meal. Sherry said to take all the money that we saved by not having an elaborate funeral and cater a big beautiful luncheon or dinner. So that's what we're going to do."

We sat for over an hour, and people continued sharing their memories of Sherry along with some quiet tears. Then the hospice nurse arrived and filled out the necessary paperwork for the death certificate. I left after that with everyone still sitting in Sherry's room.

A CELEBRATION OF LIFE

Sherry died Sunday evening. On Wednesday morning her memorial service took place at a nearby community center.

The auditorium was filled. There were two to three hundred people. Dave spoke first and then introduced me. I walked up to the podium and said, "As I sat with Sherry through her dying process, she asked that this memorial service be called 'A Celebration of Life.' She said to tell you, 'I know some of you are grieving, but I want this to be about the good things that have come out of my being here on earth.' So, as Sherry wished, this time together will give each of us an opportunity to open our hearts and say anything we wish to say.

"I would like to begin by saying that in the last week of her life, Sherry left her family and friends a legacy of how we can experience death differently, with more awareness and with more compassion.

"It is important for us to explore how her death affected us, first in our perceptions of dying, and secondly in our attitudes about living from now on.

"Since my own near-death experience twenty years ago, I have been helping people die. I have come to believe that death is a natural part of the web of life, and I am committed to helping the dying and their families find ways to transform their suffering into something transcendent and healing. Suffering can be transformed. Sherry proved that. First, she accepted her undeniable condition, and with that acceptance she began a transformation. Miraculously, fear, anger and pain became love, compassion and forgiveness. And Sherry's transformation also was contagious. All of us who witnessed her dying were equally transformed. These miracles of love, compassion and forgiveness quietly entered our own minds and hearts every time we touched Sherry or looked into her eyes.

"Finally, with Sherry's deep belief in a continuing existence after her death, she reminded us that 'though we may be born in time, we are nourished in eternity.'"

Next, Sherry's father and uncle chanted prayers in Hebrew. Then her father again recited the Elizabeth Barrett Browning poem. Lisa talked eloquently about her best friend, Sherry, and even found humor to share about the folding of the towels and sheets. She helped us to chuckle with a humorous story of the dilemma in the stacking of Sherry's dishwasher. Other friends and family shared their feelings about Sherry for over two hours, then we were directed into a large social hall where an elegant meal was served. The first thing I saw as I walked in was a table filled with "mounds and mounds of shrimp." So this was the meaning of Sherry's vision of shrimp! Two hundred or more people sat down together and shared a meal in honor of Sherry. I hoped she was watching.

Later, as I got into my car to return to my office, I turned on the radio and Billy Joel was singing "Only the Good Die Young." *Now I know you're here, Sherry,* I thought to myself.

"All right!" I said out loud to her with a smile on my face.

I peacefully drove to my office, thanking God and Sherry Rosen for the privilege of what I had experienced over the last week.

It is now a year since Sherry died. It has taken me this year to be able to step back and begin to realize the impact that Sherry's dying process has had on me. I am grateful to have participated in it with her. Although I never knew Sherry before, she opened herself to me and allowed me into her personal world during her beautiful and naturally spiritual journey at her life's end. She allowed me to watch her transformation from a pained and fearful human into a spiritual being full of forgiveness, peace, grace and love. Sherry had been wounded and traumatized early in her childhood, and then those scars had bound her heart. Her illness, and the fact that it was terminal, gave her an opportunity to explore her own beliefs about love and spirituality. Sherry explained to me that during this time she never gave herself limits by adhering to one thought system but explored her own feelings about what it is to be a spiritual being.

I believe a lifetime of healing came for Sherry from the powerful prayer service in her living room just above us. It healed her in ways we can understand and probably some ways beyond our human comprehension. First, a physical healing of sorts occurred when she vomited and relieved herself of painful pressure in her abdomen. I then realized that her pain medication wasn't working and was able to obtain a more effective prescription from her doctor. There is also wonderful symbolism here about her heart being relieved of pressure and pain. And as her subsequent acts proved, her heart was able to open and forgive, allowing everyone in.

At the same time, we heard her father's beautiful reciting of the poem "How do I love thee? Let me count the ways." The poem ends:

> Smiles, tears, of all my life!—and if God choose,
> I shall but love thee better after death.

With that last line of the poem, Sherry's father was telling her that he loved her enough to let her go.

From a spiritual standpoint, the energy of God moved in with remarkable synchronicities, including the powerful scenes in *Steel Magnolias* where parent Sally Field watches her child die and then grieves after the funeral. I was startled when I recognized this scene on Sherry's television, and I was going to change it quickly, but Sherry said, "No, leave it on." She took it all in. Then we watched her childhood home movies. There she saw the love surrounding her in her childhood, and we talked a little about it. With her heart now opened, Sherry was able to release painful memories. After I left, Sherry was able to invite her entire family to join her in the last twenty-four hours of her life. Sherry's heart had opened to the point where there were no longer good relatives or bad relatives. She shared her love with everyone who surrounded her in the waiting process. Sherry made room in her heart for the forgiveness that was so desperately needed for her to share the final passage at her life's end.

Sherry died with grace and serenity, and this has had a healing impact on all of us. We carry Sherry's message of love and forgiveness in our hearts. Because she let everyone in at the very end of her life, Sherry showed us that it is never too late to take fear and pain and transform them into forgiveness and love

NOTES FOR CAREGIVERS

My role as a visiting caregiver is much easier than that of the close or primary caregiver, who is often the significant other and living, painfully, through this process of escalating illness and dying, twenty-four hours a day. I mentioned in Sherry's story that after our all-night vigil, I felt I had "shrunk" inside to make "room" for Sherry. I was able to leave and go home—take a bath and relax in my own bed. Many times, you are at home and sharing your bed with the person who you are helping die. There is no place to go to get your *self* back.

I often counsel primary caregivers during their loved one's final passage and after it is over. A common thread of loss of self continues through every caregiver's story.

There are local support groups for caregivers in every large city and even in small towns. Local cancer societies can refer you to one near you. If you can't leave home and you are on the Internet, there are now support groups online. They help. Self-care is important.

Many times primary caregivers are afraid to complain—feeling guilty or selfish—for a number of reasons that only continue to damage them inside. Of course we want to be everything we can be to our dying loved ones. But we are still human and have needs. We forget that we, too, are losing our partners, or parents, or friends—so part of us is dying, too. If others offer to help, allow them to. Leave when you can, even if it is to take a walk or sit in a park.

Caregivers may find themselves "entrained" during the dying process to the extent that they go through the beginning of the journey with the dying person. Dave, Lisa and I experienced the spiritual peace that Sherry was feeling. As her being became less physical and more spiritual, the power of her spirit entrained us. We were fortunate to experience this state for the entire weekend. Dave said he continued to experience it for several days after. When he and I sat up all night watching Sherry breathe, we soon were breathing in the same pattern she was. We were experiencing entrainment. Perhaps entrainment is best explained by the example of tuning forks or clocks. When one tuning fork is struck and it vibrates, soon the other tuning forks nearby will also begin to vibrate. If you have several clocks with pendulums in a room—and you start all the pendulums swinging at different times—when you later return to the room, all the pendulums will be swinging in sync. These are examples of entrainment.

So, too, can we experience entrainment. Be aware that in your deepest grief during the loss of a loved one, there may be moments with a sense of being timeless when a deep sense of spiritual communion with your dying loved one is possible.

People taking morphine or any painkiller, and dying, may perceive reality through a fog of varying degrees, depending on any number of factors. Even without drugs, they are sometimes moving back and forth between here and other realities or levels of consciousness. Sherry was awake, but I could tell that her orientation to this reality was becoming more veiled. To truly communicate, I needed to be a few inches away from her, making total eye contact. Or I would massage her feet and look directly at her. So move in close to the dying person and make plenty of eye contact.

Physical touch and energy work are excellent ways to help relieve pain and fear. The hands-on work we did with Sherry is easy. What I love first about these hands-on meditations is they help the dying relax. Coloring improves and often the dying tell me that their pain medication is working. Second, hands-on work gives caregivers a chance to easily give love. At times I have even observed this technique giving caregivers the same feeling of peace as their loved ones and a sense of connection that borders on entrainment.

I will continue sharing stories of physical touch and energy work for the dying throughout this book. Another excellent book to assist you in this work is *Your Healing Hands* by Richard Gordon.

THREE

Loyalty:
My Father's Story

*A*s I helped others go through the death and mourning of their parents, I was aware that my own parents would not live forever. Occasionally I realized that I, too, would have to go through this gut-wrenching process. I knew that no matter how many people I helped, no matter how many workshops I conducted or books I wrote, nothing could prepare me for experiencing my own father's death. I tried not to think about it.

The story of my father's death begins with one phone call. The phone rang one Wednesday evening after I had returned from my office to my home in Baltimore, Maryland. It was my brother's wife, Eunice, and she quickly told me that she had just received a call from a physician in Florida who had admitted my father to the hospital. He had diagnosed acute leukemia and believed my dad would die within a few days, a week at the most. A crushing blow moved over me, making me feel pressure from everywhere—inside and out. Charlie Whitfield and I weren't married yet, but we had been living together for a short while. That day he was out of town presenting a workshop based on his best-selling book, *Healing the Child Within*. Charlie is also a physician and could have helped me sort out what little information I had about my father's condition. He wouldn't be coming home that night, and for the first (and only) time, I didn't have the number of the hotel where he could be reached in Seattle. I was alone with my pain, my fear, my sorrow. I called my friend Mary Ellen in Connecticut. When she picked up, I said, "My father is going to die!" And then I couldn't say another word. I couldn't breathe. She listened as I gasped and then finally sobbed. After I sobbed, I could talk again, and I gave her what few details I had. Mary Ellen helped me plan my next step.

I was scheduled to give a workshop the next day and decided that afterward I would fly to Florida. My horror at the realization that my dad was leaving here first and that I would have to deal with the overwhelming problems of moving my mother was just too much for me to comprehend. My mother was always so needy. I would try not to think about her needs.

My workshop the next day was at the Baltimore School of Massage. Twenty massage therapists were attending, and some had signed up two or three months earlier. I couldn't cancel the workshop. I kept up a dialogue with my father as I got dressed: "Don't die, Daddy. Don't die. I promise I'll get there late tonight. Please hold on."

I told the workshop attendees right away the tragic turn my life had taken the night before. I could see by the looks on their faces that they were all there for me. I had entitled this workshop "Helping to Heal the Child Within—The Emotional and Spiritual Connection in Breath and Body Work." With a topic like that, and with massage therapists as an audience, I couldn't have had a kinder or more compassionate group. As I taught them, they helped me get through the day.

At 7:30 P.M. I was on a plane for Florida and arrived in Ft. Lauderdale at 10:00 P.M. I prayed the entire time, repeating the words of my prayer over and over, like a mantra, to keep my mind from imagining the pain I was about to go through. I had said the first part of my prayer thousands of times before this night, each and every time I gave a talk or put my hands on a client or patient: "Dear God, Dear Spirit, please may I be an instrument of your healing energy. Please help me to get out of the way so that you may come through." On the plane that night, I added: "Oh, please help my family. Please surround us with your love and healing energy." None of my work helping others to die could help me right now. I felt like I was a little girl again and I was going to say good-bye to my daddy.

My mother and daughter Beth were there to greet me. Within fifteen minutes my brother Marshall landed from Detroit and ten minutes later my son Gary joined us from Connecticut. It pleased us to see each other and comforted us to the point that for a few minutes we almost could have forgotten what lay ahead, except my mother looked so bad, and Beth was so stressed.

Gary went home with Beth. Marshall and I went with our mother. I don't remember that night. I was numb. I think we tried to get information from our mother about our father's condition and at the same time find out from her if he had left instructions or a file of important papers. I think she got angry, and we backed off and went to bed. It's hard to remember anything clearly when I'm numb, but numb can be a useful feeling. It helps us to survive and to continue functioning through horrendous times.

The next morning we were up and dressed at 7:00 A.M., and since we weren't allowed into the hospital ICU until 9:00, the three of us went to a restaurant for breakfast. As we sat in a booth I heard the music playing overhead from a local radio station. It was Whitney Houston singing "One Moment in

Time." Little did I know that I was soon to have *my* one moment in time.

My mother sat across from Marshall and me. She looked at him with the same fuzzy gaze I had seen on her face all my life. "What is it you do again?" she asked.

Marshall said, "Mom! For thirty-one years I've been teaching school to tough kids. Many have been abused, physically and in other ways."

"Who would do that to a child?" my mother asked.

There was an uncomfortable silence as Marshall and I looked at each other. The truth is, my mother had repeatedly abused my brother and me, but we had never told anyone, nor had we confronted her about it. We knew she had had an abusive childhood herself.

After a moment or two, my mother looked at us and asked again, "Who would do such a thing?"

I looked at her and realized this was my chance to finally talk about it out loud. I said, "Mother, you physically abused us when we were kids. You abused Marshall and me, often."

She stared off into space and then blinked a few times. I could see her struggle to connect with what I had just said. Then she said, so quietly that I had to strain to hear, "I'm sorry."

And that was it. It was over. In one sentence, *one moment in time,* it was over. My mother and I finished our unfinished business. We released each other. And, for that one moment, I sensed that our souls recognized each other.

Later, as I drove us to the hospital in my father's car, I was grateful for the last couple of years I had had with him. We had finally gotten to know each other. My father had always been distant. Either he hadn't talked at all or he had lectured, using words like a wall that kept us apart. However, less than two years ago he had called me long distance and actually pleaded for me to come and be with him. My mother was once again in intensive care, and he was sure that this time it was worse and she might die. I was on the next plane to Florida, curious to be with him without her there and scared because I wasn't sure what he would be like.

My father and I had our ups and our downs during that visit, but we talked—really talked—and I finally got to know him. The first night we were together, after we came back from visiting my mother in the ICU, I played a videotape that I had brought to show my dad. He hadn't met Charlie yet, and I wanted him to understand a little of what Charlie did. The tape was one of several tapes that covered a two-day workshop on Charlie's book *Healing the Child Within*. I hadn't paid much attention to titles as I pulled a tape off the shelf and packed it, but ironically it was the one on core issues in recovery. There are about fifteen core issues ranging from fear of abandonment, inability to trust, all-or-none thinking and behaving, and high tolerance for inappropriate behavior to difficulty resolving conflict, difficulty giving and receiving love, over-responsibility for others, and neglecting our own needs.

Dad and I were sitting on the sofa in front of the TV. I hit the start button and there was Charlie, teaching about fear of abandonment and how it affects us.

"That's my issue. Fear of abandonment. My whole life," Dad said.

"What?" I asked. My dad had never revealed his story to me, and now I was watching him open up right before my eyes.

When I was young, my dad looked like Humphrey Bogart, but as he got older he looked more and more like Edward G.

Robinson. I used to catch a glimpse of him every so often driving his van right past me when he was making deliveries in our town. Dad was always driving with a cigarette in his mouth, and that made me laugh. He had "quit" smoking years earlier, according to my mother. But dad was in the vending machine business, candy and cigarettes, and I had wondered how he could quit when he had them right there in the van. He hadn't. He quit smoking in front of my mother, but out on the open road he smoked, looking more and more like Edward G. Robinson, although as he told his story to me now, I could glimpse Humphrey Bogart again.

"Fear of abandonment. Tell Charlie that's my issue. Ever since I was a little boy. My dad left when I was six. No one told me he was in Herman Kiefer Hospital for a whole year. They just told me when he died. I was seven. He died of TB."

My heart did a flip-flop.

"So I didn't have a father. A lot of the other kids only had one parent. My mother did a pretty good job raising me and my two sisters, but then she died when I was sixteen. I quit school and worked to keep us together in this little apartment. We still had some of the beautiful things my parents were able to carry from Russia when they moved here during the Bolshevik Revolution. And one day, I came home from work and everything was gone. The place was empty. My sister had sold everything to have enough money to leave town and follow her dreams. There I was in an empty place—abandoned."

I was frozen for a second or two. I looked at my father with sudden compassion. I knew that something huge had happened to him, but I never knew what because he would never talk about himself.

"Daddy, that's so sad. I never knew. You were so young to lose your father and then your mother."

One evening a few of his cousins who lived in the same retirement complex came over and we sat and talked. They wanted to talk about my mother and how she dominated my father and kept them all away. I was listening to others finally speak the truth about my family.

I heard them talking about a lawsuit that was brought against my mother in Michigan a few years earlier before they moved to Florida. My mother actually hit a small child who was pulling on the knobs of one of my father's vending machines. All my life, I had kept the family secret of her abusive treatment of my brother and me, and now I was hearing this.

"That's terrible!" I announced.

"Oh, Barbie!" Dad said. "You know your mother. You know the way she is! Most of the time she's okay. She thought the boy was going to break my machine. She was so angry about the other ones that had been broken. She doesn't mean any harm, she just doesn't know how." He stopped speaking and looked down. Perhaps for the first time, I saw my father not just as a parent, but as a man who dedicated his life to taking care of my mother. He did this not only for her, but for us. He knew that if he left, he would abandon us to her rage. I had often wondered why my dad hadn't stopped my mother when she flew off into a rage and hit us. Now I realized that my father had protected us the only way he knew how—by staying. We were young, and he was afraid she would destroy my brother and me. And he could never have gotten custody of us. Even if she had been addicted to pills, back in the 1950s the courts always gave the children to the mother. "And besides," my father said, raising his hand up over his head and looking very much like Tevye in *Fiddler on the Roof,* "I *love* her!"

I couldn't take that away from him. He had always loved

her, and I know that in her own way she had always loved him, too.

I drove to the hospital grateful for that visit and for subsequent ones when we were all together. I was grateful, too, for the new closeness I felt with my dad. He and I would go off somewhere beyond the range of my mother's ears and we would reminisce. Sometimes he told me stories I had never heard before, and he even shared one of his favorite memories with me.

"One of the best memories your mother and I have was just a few years ago when you were living in Connecticut. Remember, we came up for Christmas and Mary Ellen's folks invited us over for Christmas Eve? Your mother and I have never seen such a big family—seven kids and all those wonderful grandkids."

"Remember, Daddy," I said, "when I pulled up to their drive, Mom wanted to know if it was a single-family dwelling?"

"Well, you know," my dad replied, "not many couples stay in the house they raised their kids in. And the Dohertys had such a large family that they needed that big house. Remember it had just snowed, and with all the colored lights decorating their house, why, I felt like we were in a Bing Crosby Christmas movie. It was a wonderful evening. They took us in just like we were old friends."

"And you sure held your own with the judge, Dad," I laughed. "You and Jim went on all evening about baseball."

"Well, minor league baseball was real big in the 1930s. Jim knew his stuff."

"And so did you!" I replied.

I remembered wondering that evening as we drove to the Dohertys' house in Hamden, just beyond New Haven, what my parents could have in common to talk about with an edu-cated judge and his family. The house was filled when we got there—seven children and their mates, twenty-seven or so grandchildren, and one or two great-grandchildren. I had lost count. May Doherty had been so gracious to my mother. Then we watched her sit by their huge Christmas tree giving out gifts to everyone. She even had little presents for both my parents. My mom and dad brought them a gift, too. It was a china plate that said, "God Bless the Irish." And the whole time, Jim and my father sat in a far corner in the big living room talking baseball. Jim had played in the minors so he knew about everyone back then. The surprise for me was my dad. He kept right up with the conversation. Those baseball games were sixty years earlier, but they remembered them like it was yesterday.

The best memory I have of my parents is of the last time we were all together in Key West for my son Steven's wedding. It was only five months earlier, and we stayed at a wonderful little hotel called "The Banyan Tree." My whole family—my children, parents, brother, Charlie and I—were together for three days, and of course there was much joy over the wed-ding celebration.

Steven is the music teacher at Key West High School. He married Robin, the music teacher from Sugarloaf Elementary School three islands away. A four-star restaurant catered the party. The wedding took place in a garden behind the oldest house on Key West on a hot, tropical June afternoon. It had been raining all week, but the rains stopped and the blue sky brought even more joy for all of us. My parents were beaming: their first grandchild was getting married. The outdoor wed-ding ended at 5:00, but there was so much food left over that we brought it back to the hotel and set it up in our room. All of Robin and Steve's friends came back to our resort, went swimming and then ate again, so the wedding celebration continued late into the night. We got to meet and know friends of my children that we hadn't met before. Most of them were music teachers, too. The next afternoon, Beth, Charlie and I took the rest of the food (there was still plenty) over to the Salvation Army where it was used for the evening meal. Later that evening, we walked to the southernmost point on the island, which is also the southernmost point of the United States, and watched a glorious orange, pink and purple sunset.

After the wedding, I had noticed that my parents both looked bad. A few days later my mother's doctor put her on dialysis. I figured my dad was tired because my mother was getting sicker. He didn't complain, he continued working thirty hours a week, and he also took my mother for dialysis three times a week. No one knew he was sick until he came home from work one night and quietly collapsed. My mother had called 911 and an ambulance took my father to the nearest emergency room. By the time I got to the hospital, I realized that the doctor who was treating my father didn't know the histories of either of my parents, and my mother hadn't had dialysis in three days.

As Marshall, my mother and I walked into the ICU, the nurse at the desk dialed the doctor in charge of my dad's case. He carefully went over lab reports with me. He also explained his frustration at not having known my father before, at having no history to go on, and at how severe my father's leukemia had become. He apologized for not being able to do more and said he might have been able to do something if this had been caught earlier. Finally, he told me that my dad was in a deep coma and that he would probably die that day or the next. I couldn't feel my legs as I walked toward my father's room. My brother stood at the door unable to stay inside. "Forgive me, Barbara," he pleaded. "You've always had the stomach for all this, but I can't take it. I'll be in the hall nearby if you need me."

I walked in. "Oh, Daddy!" I cried, and I brushed his hair from his forehead. "Oh, Daddy! I love you. I'm so sorry this is happening. I love you, Daddy." I must have stood there for close to half an hour talking to him, crying and stroking his hair. I couldn't touch his arms—they were all black and blue from the restraints and his disease. Suddenly he opened his eyes and sweetly said, "Hello," and then asked me, "Am I dead yet?" I would have smiled but my mother was yelling at him, "Shut up, Julius. You're not going to die!"

My father started thrashing, trying to kick off the covers and pull out the tubes and needles. A nurse came in and tried to get him to swallow a tranquilizer. As I worked with her he knocked over some fluid and it spilled all over me. Remarkably, he still had all the physical strength he had possessed—the strength that those who knew him had seen—throughout his lifetime. At one point, he drifted off to sleep and I asked my mother when she had last had dialysis. She didn't remember. She didn't know her doctor's name or where she received dialysis.

I went out to the nurse and asked for the name of the nephrologist on call and then went through the politics of getting my mother her treatment. As luck would have it, she could be dialyzed on the same floor we were on.

She refused dialysis at first, when I said I was getting her help. It hit me that she might be on to something. Her husband was her whole life, and now he was dying. If she refused dialysis, she would die, too. Maybe she wanted to. I thought about how much they loved each other and that this could be a peaceful way for the two of them to pass through together. I carefully explained this to her.

She started screaming, "Daddy is not dying!"

I sat with her eye to eye, explaining to her several times, "Dad has a blood disease that he never complained about and didn't even know he had, and now he is at the end. He is going to die, and you have to stop screaming at him not to talk about it. He may wake up again, and all three of my kids are coming, and this is our chance—and yours—to say all we need to say."

She then announced, "I want my dialysis. I have no intention of dying!" She was out the door and in treatment within three minutes.

It took my father only a day to die. I massaged his feet every chance I could, and he would open his eyes and gaze into mine whenever I did. "I love you, Daddy!" I would tell him. And in my heart I would also tell him it was okay to go to the Light. I couldn't say that out loud, and I don't know why. Maybe it was too much responsibility, or maybe saying it out loud would have stripped me of my last vestige of denial.

Suddenly, my father said very clearly, "I see my Mumma. She's here. But I know she's dead."

"I think she has come to help you, to help take you with her," I answered. My heart was crying. The pressure in my chest was overwhelming. I was also relieved. His mother was here to help him. I was so grateful. I felt a great deal of responsibility being lifted from my shoulders.

"Daddy, I'm so glad she's here for you. See, you can't die alone. No one is alone when they die. We always get helpers from the other side. We're here with you now, but even if we weren't, you would have your Mumma." I had never heard him talk of his mother as "Mumma." He said it in such an endearing way. I was suddenly happy for him. She had died when he was only a teenager and now, in his seventies, he had her back.

"How can she be here? She's been dead for so long."

"Daddy, remember my near-death experience? Mother's mother came for me, remember? Bubbie came."

"Oh, yeah!" my dad said. "Can you see my Mumma, too?"

"No, Dad. But I can feel her. I can feel her presence." And I could.

I had been named for Dad's mother. I knew from a few old pictures that I looked like her, too. And now, somehow we were together, linked through my father. I felt calm for the first time since that phone call telling me he was ill. I looked at his face. He was a child again with his Mumma. And in my heart I had the courage to let him go.

I stroked his hair off his forehead. "Rest now, Daddy. I'm going in the hall to get Marshall."

My brother came in and leaned over the bed for a second and talked gently. But then a technician came in and started to work on Dad's arm to take blood. Things started to fly. Dad was trying to push everyone away. He was pulling out tubes. His wedding ring flew across the room. The most remarkable fact in this bizarre scene was that he was in restraints. I don't know how he could do all that. When I worked in ICU, a patient in restraints could sometimes grab us, but I never saw anything like this.

A nurse came in. We were all trying to restrain him while she forced a pill in his mouth.

"This will calm you down," she said.

"Leave me alone!" he yelled. "Leave me alone! Just let me be! Mumma! Mumma!"

"Why are you drawing blood?" I asked her.

She said, "That is one of the few procedures his doctors will continue to do while he is dying, to check his blood sugar and keep it in balance."

"Why is he getting IVs?" I asked, raising my voice so the nurse could hear me over Dad's screams. "IVs mean you have to keep him in restraints. He should be free of all this.

"What difference does his blood sugar mean now? He deserves to die in peace. I want all the tubes out and no more tests."

The nurse looked at me and spoke quietly, with compassion. "I'm not supposed to be saying this, so please don't let on that I said anything, but I think your father would be much more comfortable at a hospice."

My mind was going a million miles an hour. *I should know that. I tell people that. Why didn't I do something?* I said to myself. *Barbara, knock it off. You can't be objective right now. This is your father. Just let other people help you now.* I looked this nurse deeply in the eyes and said, "Oh, thank you! I know you're right. Please tell me what the procedure is here. How do I get him to a hospice?"

"I'm going to call the social worker from this unit. She can call a hospice. Good luck!"

My father had settled down. Marshall looked green. "Come on," I suggested. "Let's go talk in the hall." We walked outside the room, and I told my brother what I wanted to do. He quickly agreed when I explained to him that our dad would be much more comfortable in a hospice. Hospitals are set up to do everything they can to sustain life. They would continue to insert tubes and take blood. My father didn't want or need that now. Hospice would concentrate on helping to keep him comfortable.

We looked in on our father. He was sleeping soundly. Our mother wouldn't be back from dialysis for an hour. I left word at the desk for my kids if they came in. Marshall and I went for a walk in the warm Florida sunshine.

When we came back, our mother was back in the room. She was weak from three hours of dialysis, but her coloring looked healthier. Beth and Gary had come into the room.

Occasionally, one or both would cry. Dad would open his eyes and tell us about seeing his mother. If he asked whether he was dead yet, Mom would scream at him, "Shut up, Julius!" and I would gently, but firmly, tell her to stop.

My dad quieted down. Then he gave me instructions about how to handle the money he was leaving and told me how to take care of Mother. My heart did a "double sink." Dad asked for my son Steve. He wanted to see Steve before he died. And then in walked Steven, who had been driving for five hours from Key West. Dad took one look at him and burst out crying. His eyes were riveted on Steve. Both of them were crying. So was I, to the point where I had to look away, but then I had to glance back because there was so much beauty between them. These two men had loved each other from the moment of Steven's birth, or maybe before. Their love had always been unconditional—grandfather and grandson—two souls nurturing each other through the ups and downs of life. They had a strong resemblance. When Steven was a baby he looked like my father's baby pictures. Now, Steve's wife Robin was pregnant.

"Name the baby after me," Dad sobbed. According to Jewish tradition, a baby cannot be named after a living person. A baby is named after a deceased loved one. Steven was crying. We were all crying.

Dad told Steven, "Steve, remember how I used to call you

Stevarino? Or just my little Steve-o. You were so little. You painted me the cutest pictures. I think I saved them all."

"Yeah, Grandpa! You know, I think my very first memory is of your van. I remember how you'd pull up the drive and let all the kids we played with go inside and get a candy bar. Boy, I felt like the richest kid in the world."

"You and your friends were so little I had to lift each one of you up and into the van. Your legs were too short to make the step."

Beth was swaying in time with her little rendition of "The Candy Man" song. She had sung that song to her grandfather, Julius, ever since I could remember.

Gary chimed in. "We all thought of you as the Candy Man, Grandpa. All my friends called you the Candy Man!" His body was moving back and forth with Beth's.

I watched my father transform. No longer the dying old man, he was now their grandfather again, with a look of love framed in his stern, Old World face. It was a special look I had often wondered about. And my kids were softly chatting with him as though it was a regular day and we were on an outing together. Beth reminded her grandfather of a moment in her memory when he was especially kind. She had broken her arm and he brought her a teddy bear in the hospital.

Beth, Steven and Gary together told him, "I love you, Grandpa!" Then they thanked him for all his love.

He looked deeply into my face and told me how much he appreciated keeping his extra vending machines in our garage. When he would come to work on them I would cook his favorite foods. And I reminded him of one of those visits when I blocked the doorway and wouldn't let him leave until he kissed me.

My brother was remembering a Passover dinner when he

had invited several nuns from the university where he taught to join the family. Our father, though a little bit surprised when he came in, was charming to them, and they always asked Marshall about him after that. Dad just grinned.

We all glowed, basking in great memories. And my dad looked at all the beauty in the beaming faces around him and said, "You know what I would love right now?"

"What?" We all chimed in.

"Corned beef," he replied. "I would love a corned beef sandwich."

Beth and Gary took off in search of the closest deli. The hospice nurse arrived and spent a while going over the hospital records. She asked my mother a few questions and was told to ask me. The two of us went over Dad's condition and agreed that hospice was appropriate. She explained that he was eligible with his insurance and then asked if I had any questions. I briefly explained, while trying to handle my own pain, that my mother was in denial and I didn't know how we could handle her.

The hospice nurse was great with my mother. I watched her explain all the facts of my father's situation with clarity and gentleness. A tear came into my mom's eye as she asked, "If he gets better can he come home?"

"Absolutely!" the nurse answered, and she brought out a lot of papers for us to go through and sign. This nurse was exceptional in the way she handled all of us. For a split second, I could break out of my pain and be proud that I was part of the hospice movement.

Beth and Gary came back with seven corned beef sandwiches. There was room for four of us to get close with my dad on the bed. Two had to sit on chairs. No one from the hospital staff came in. We "broke bread" together and chomped on pickles. In our own way, we were sharing a communion—not with a wafer—but with corned beef. The act of communion is so sacred. This felt sacred, too, and the corned beef added a level of humor that we all noticed and needed. To this day, my children and I still talk about Grandpa and the corned beef sandwiches.

Two ambulance attendants came to transfer Dad to the hospice. My father's face registered that they were two cute and young blond women. His face lit up. My brother rode in the ambulance and proudly told me later "Dad is still being Dad. He kibitzed all the way there." I drove in Dad's car following closely behind. My mom talked nonstop, but her voice barely registered. Through the small window in the back of the ambulance I could see the top of my father's head. The attendants had the stretcher in a sitting position so he could breathe easier. As we pulled into the hospice's parking lot, a voice inside me screamed with denial. Though I looked and acted calm, I was realizing the gravity and finality behind moving him to a hospice.

Although I'd been in many hospices before, I walked in and saw this hospice differently, because now it was one of my loved ones who was being admitted. As I gave all the insurance information to a soft-spoken man behind a desk, I watched a group of grieving people who were just leaving. The admitting clerk gave me back my father's ID cards and told me how to find my father's room. Walking down the long hall, I looked in each room. I saw gravely ill people. I wanted to grab my father, mother and brother. I wanted to take them and run.

I walked into the room I had been directed to, bracing myself for the worst. Instead, my eyes and heart jumped as I witnessed my father being cradled by a nurse as she sponge-bathed his shoulders and back. Then another nurse gently gave him a dose of liquid morphine and he willingly swallowed it. There were no tubes, no needles. His bed had some padding around the sides that came up so he wouldn't hurt himself. There were no restraints. One nurse explained to me, "He can have the morphine every two to four hours depending on his level of anxiety and pain." She looked deeply into my eyes and said, "You look exhausted. You can stay as long as you want, but you really need some rest."

At 11:00 P.M. my mom and Marshall told me that they needed to go back to my parents' apartment and rest. I knew my way around the city, having lived in the area several years earlier, and I had to drive them. I have gone back to this moment hundreds of times since. I knew deep in my soul that my father could die that night. I massaged his feet one last time. He opened his eyes, and I told him I loved him and that he had been a good father. And I left him. I could have driven back to the hospice, but I couldn't find the strength. Marshall and my mother went into the two bedrooms, and I crashed on the living room sofa. I was out.

Around 3:25 A.M., I was awakened by the sound of someone breathing. I looked up to see who it was, but no one was there. Then, the breathing simply stopped, and within a few seconds the phone rang. It was the hospice. My father had just died, and I knew I had heard him take his last breath. I was too drained to go back to him, so he had come to me. At that moment I was happy for him. He was finally home. He was with his Mumma. No more pain. I thanked God. I asked this energy we call God to take my father in. But I knew in my heart that God already had.

I woke my mother and Marshall and told them that Dad had died. Then, according to my father's instructions, I picked

the Eternal Light Funeral Home out of the yellow pages because they advertised "discount funerals." Gary went with me
in the morning to pick out the casket. My father had said to
buy "the cheapest," but I just couldn't do it. So instead I
picked the second cheapest one. We skipped a service in a
chapel and had a graveside service instead. I asked Rabbi
Green, who the funeral home sent, to invite anyone to speak
who wanted to because he didn't know my father.

It was a beautiful sunny December day in Ft. Lauderdale as
our family gathered. We left the cars at the entrance to the
cemetery and walked to his grave. I scanned the beauty of this
memorial park. Gary and I had done a good job. Upon Dad's
request, we may have skimped on the casket and other small
items at the funeral home, but we had also visited cemeteries
and knew as soon as we saw this one to stop looking. It was
more expensive, so I said in my heart as we walked, "Sorry,
Dad. I can't just put you anywhere! This is beautiful. No head-
stones standing up in rows. This is more like a park. And
there's a nursery on the other side of the fence that I thought
you would appreciate." My dad loved to work in his garden
when we were kids. I think it was his way of escaping, or
maybe he was meditating.

Mother, Marshall, his wife Eunice and I sat in front of my
father's casket. Our children stood beside and behind us.
Rabbi Jacob Green stood on the other side of the casket facing
us. He was very tall and spoke very loudly as though there
were a hundred people behind us. In fact, I don't think there
were even twenty people there plus a few workers from the
cemetery. Even so, I barely heard the rabbi speaking. I stood
with Marshall and our mother and recited the Hebrew prayer
for the dead. "Yisgadal veyiskadash . . ."

Rabbi Green invited anyone to speak who wished to, and I

watched and listened in amazement through a narrow window of sorrow.

I watched my son Gary walk to the head of my father's casket.

"Grandpa would take me with him in his van to fill his machines from the time I was a little boy. Wherever we went people's faces would light up when they saw him. Everyone loved Grandpa Julius. Wherever we would go."

Beth walked up and through a trembling voice said, "Grandpa, I'll miss our weekly dinners . . ." and she couldn't finish.

My niece Terri talked about his stern looks and loving smile.

Another niece, Brenda, said, "Grandpa, the second your van turned the corner and drove toward our house, my heart would jump. That is the earliest memory I have—of you coming to be with us."

Steven and Robin stood together and Steve talked first. "Grandpa, you taught me how to trust in myself. You showed me how to work hard. Your work ethics were a perfect role model for the way I try to be."

Robin said, "I'll miss you, Grandpa Julius. I didn't know you long but you were very loving."

Finally, my niece Laurie stood. Crying, she said, "Grandpa, I always took for granted that you would be here to share my milestones with me; my graduation from college, my wedding. I just knew you would be with me. Even though you've died, I know you're going to be with me, always."

I kept thinking how proud Dad would be. I remembered my NDE, and I knew that he was proud. I had to keep reminding myself that he was probably here with us, but realizing that didn't help because I was thinking of myself and I wanted him back.

As I finish writing this story of my father's death, I am aware of "The Candy Man" song playing in my mind. It won't go away. But that's all right. I am feeling my sadness, and this music connects me to it and to him.

A NOTE TO LOVED ONES

On the day my father died I had a stark realization. As the day wore on I realized that I—and possibly my family—was functioning and perceiving differently. This is an altered state of consciousness where time seems to stop and the voices and feelings of our inner life become louder and clearer. Transpersonal therapist and author John Welwood calls this state of consciousness "unconditional presence." It is a heightened sense of reality. He says that when the heart breaks out of its shell, we feel raw and vulnerable. This is the beginning of feeling real compassion for ourselves, because we slow down and authentically see and feel our distress having an impact on us. Then our pain can awaken our desire and will to live in a new way. When we open to this awareness, it becomes unconditional presence, just being with what is happening in our inner life right now, without any agenda.

My heart was breaking because I was losing my father. At the same time I catapulted into this heightened state of awareness. Time had stopped. *A Course in Miracles* calls such an experience the "Holy Instant." Eastern mysticism calls it "being in the Tao." Every step my feet took registered profoundly. The scenes I viewed in the hospital appeared like virtual reality. Eye contact with another took me directly into that person's being. Each person I connected with knew easily what I was conveying. My connection with my father was total—or more than I had ever realized was possible.

When my father was conscious and with me, he too was in

this state. Knowing about unconditional presence made it easier for us to "move in" to the situation and take full advantage of it, so our final moments together, although filled with sadness, could be the best possible.

FOUR

Wounded:
My Mother's Story

I share this story because there are so many people who have suffered through a parent's death in a similar way. Perhaps this story will help them.

While my father's death happened in almost the easiest way a sudden death can occur, a year and a month later my mother's death showed how painfully helpless we can be. But even in our helplessness we can respect the dying person and at the same time honor our own feelings as they come up. In both my father's and mother's stories, their dysfunctional backgrounds had included a lack of communication. My mother's denial and need to control hung like a thick fog over any attempts we had ever made to talk.

The story I am about to tell is different from any other dying process in which I have participated. My role as a clinician or friend during the process of dying is usually that of a facilitator—I help people to communicate with each other and with Spirit.

But this time, I was simply the daughter of a dying woman who had spent most of her life lonely, angry and depressed. She had medicated herself against those feelings for as long as I could remember. Her addiction to drugs had disconnected her from herself. I believe she had actually lost touch with the essence of who she really was long ago. This loss made real communication with her impossible.

After my dad died, my brother and I felt a real sense of urgency about getting my mother to a safe, caring place where she wouldn't have to depend on us for her every need, but where we could visit her freely.

GETTING HER SETTLED

My brother Marshall and his wife Eunice tried to convince my mother to come back to Michigan with them but she wouldn't budge. Florida was her home now, she said, and she never wanted to go back to the cold winters again.

To complicate matters, I had to find another dialysis center for her. Dad had been driving my mother to a hospital an hour away for dialysis. I realized I had to quickly move those treatments to a medical center closer to where she lived. But first I had to find her an apartment that offered "assisted living." In Florida, I quickly found out that they called this a "senior hotel."

All this planning was going on while we were supposed to be "sitting *shiva*," the Jewish tradition of the family staying together and grieving for one week after a death. But I knew that if we didn't move her to a new apartment and another dialysis center soon, I would fall apart. Now I was driving her to the old dialysis center, and my father's old car was breaking down every other day. The drive was taking one-and-a-half hours. My mother, deeply depressed, did nothing to help herself.

Mother's senior healthcare provider gave me the name of an approved physician. The new doctor could fill out the forms that would transfer her to a dialysis center, and he could also supervise her care there. Eunice and I took her to an internist in North Hollywood who immediately referred us to a new nephrologist. Both of them recommended the North Park Senior Residence for assisted living. Instead of sitting *shiva*, Mother, Eunice and I went apartment hunting. We all agreed that God would forgive us!

In one afternoon, just three days after my father died, we saw an internist, a nephrologist and my parents' dentist, who had been standing ahead of us in line at the local deli. We were a little embarrassed seeing him because he asked how Dad was and we had to tell him he had just died. And we all knew, including the dentist, that we should be home sitting *shiva*. We asked him about an assisted living facility for my mother and he recommended North Park, too.

We drove up to North Park an hour later. I was happy to see that both doctors, the apartment complex, the dialysis center, the dentist and the deli were all within a mile of each other, and my daughter Beth lived about two miles away.

North Park was perfect. It had an apartment that would become available in three weeks. It had a driver and limousine that would take mother and one other resident for dialysis. It had buses to take the residents grocery shopping, to malls, parks and beaches. Once a month residents went to dinner and live shows at the hotels on the beach.

We were taken on a tour of the facility. It reminded me of a cross between a Hilton hotel and a cruise ship, although my mother was probably one of the youngest residents—and she was in her mid-seventies. It was expensive, but we told her she was worth it. I knew my father would have said it was too expensive, but I also knew he would have been proud to have provided so well for her.

We took my brother Marshall to see it. He loved it, but he

also said, "It's very expensive!" We rationalized the cost every way we could. We knew we were going to do it. There was one administrator there who was especially understanding and compassionate with Mom. Her name was Eileen and she went over everything with us. She was a young widow and could identify with my mother. My mother had two sisters, Eileen and Sylvia. She said this Eileen felt like a sister! That was it. We signed a lease.

At the end of the week, Marshall and Eunice returned to Michigan. I was left with my mother and the job of moving her and all her things, plus going through Dad's belongings. It was one of the toughest two weeks of my life. She never offered to help and did her couch potato routine instead. I was taking care of her again *and* moving her.

"Mother," I said one evening when I was packing and she was watching *Jeopardy.* "You've got to help me. I can't do this all alone. I don't know what's okay to give away and what you want to keep. Your new place is much smaller. Please help me," I asked a second time.

I had already packed all of my father's clothes and shoes. My son Steven had come over and helped me. He wore the same size as my dad, and I wanted him to have as much as he would take. It was terribly painful putting my dad's clothes in bags. I can understand better now why some of my clients leave their loved ones' clothes hanging in closets for years.

Now, for the third time, I asked my mother for help. Raising my voice, I said, "Mother, help me! You have been lying here for days and nights while I work at this. I've got the kitchen packed. The china cabinet is packed. Everything is in boxes. I am down to your personal things and then the movers are coming. Please, get up and help me with your bathroom and closet."

My mother stood up, went into the bathroom, reached for her toothbrush and walked over to the closet where she took down her overnight bag. She opened the bag and dropped her toothbrush in. She looked me right in the eye and then walked by me to the sofa. She reclined and continued watching *Jeopardy*.

I was in a state of shock. I didn't know whether to cheer because she had gotten up or scream because I now knew I was finishing her packing without her help. I walked into the large walk-in closet and started to cry. My dad had just died. Didn't she realize I had lost my father? I felt compassion for her for the loss of her husband, but she couldn't see me as a child who had lost her father.

I packed her dresses. I packed her blouses. I packed her sweaters. I knelt to pack her shoes. I remembered my life review and my mother's surgery for hammertoes. I counted thirty-two pairs of size four-and-a-half spike heels, plus five or six pairs of flats and three or four pairs of flip-flop slippers. She hadn't worn the spike heels in years; she would have fallen flat on her face if she'd tried. I packed the flats and slippers. I opened up the bags of my father's clothes that were going to a charity, and I dropped all thirty-two pairs of her spike heels into the bags, even though I had not asked her what to do with her shoes. I didn't want to be harsh, but I was so frustrated by her not helping. Finally finished, I brushed off my hands and took a long soothing bath. I slept soundly that night.

When she moved into North Park, my mother was surrounded by familiar things. I had managed to wedge into a tiny one-bedroom apartment almost everything from her much bigger condominium. I hoped it made her feel good to have her things around her. I know it made me feel better.

Just as I was finishing up getting my mother settled into her new place, everyone returned to Florida for Christmas vacation. We gathered around my mother's table for the first time at North Park, for dessert and a little housewarming. Charlie wasn't arriving until a few days later, but Marshall and Eunice, Robin and Steven, and Beth and I were there to be with our mother and grandmother. It was a sweet but somber gathering. My father's absence hung in the air, but we tried to keep the mood light by chatting about the latest happenings in the few weeks we had been apart.

"Barbara treated me terribly," my mother suddenly announced.

"What?" I said.

She looked at everyone, but not at me! "Barbara yelled at me. She raised her voice to me!"

Was she referring to her spike heels? I thought, but couldn't say out loud. I had to get up and leave the room. I retreated into the little kitchen. I held on to the sink and tried to take deep breaths. I felt like a little nine-year-old kid again after I had been bad. I was exhausted from the last two weeks, drained. I had no energy left. I was waiting for Charlie, and after he had a brief visit with Mom we were going, just the two of us, to the Keys for a week. I couldn't handle her humiliation now. I had nothing left in me.

Robin, glowing with her pregnancy and cute to begin with, walked into the kitchen, looked me in the eye and said, "Barbara, come on. You don't even have to react to that remark. We all know what she's like. You just did a great job and you should be proud. Don't let her depression get to you!"

I realized my mother still had the power to make me feel like a bad little girl. Robin brought me back into focus. And my mother didn't realize her spike heels were missing until months later.

Eileen came to visit every day and my mother talked to her. I just watched. I could never be there for my mother because she would never let me in. That was all right now. I was grateful to Eileen. I saw promise in this place. If my mother wanted to, she could extend herself and grow. I know that life's never over until we take our last breath. We are becoming who we are until we die. I watched my mother and silently cheered for her, but I couldn't help her. I had to stand back and accept what I saw and heard as she interacted with others. I felt powerless. Yet over the year that followed, I learned to stop fearing her anger and even to appreciate the beginnings of her sweetness, which was just beginning to emerge. I also learned to stand back, appreciate and let others do the jobs I normally would do.

WATCHING HER SURVIVE

After the housewarming, I left my mother at North Park, knowing that Beth would visit her a couple of times a week. I also came down to visit every chance I could. Charlie and I decided to get married the next year, and because my mother's doctors said she couldn't fly, we planned the wedding in South Florida so she could be there. She died just before we got married.

Charlie asked her a few times during the year if she thought there was a possibility she would see Julius again. She would look at Charlie, puzzled. Then one time a tear came into her eye and she said she thought so. A few times after that she told me that sometimes she could feel my father brush up against her, or see him at the foot of her bed.

When I visited I would stay the nights with Beth and spend my days with Mom. I would pick her up in the morning and take her shopping or to the beauty shop. We would go out for lunch and have dinner at North Park. We would go to the cemetery and put flowers on Dad's grave. She was furious with him for leaving her. Occasionally, she would threaten him by telling him she would be there soon and "let him have it." I asked her once if she was also angry with her father for dying when she was eleven years old. She said "absolutely" and that she had no intention of ever forgiving him. And she let me know she wasn't going to forgive Dad either.

She was sweet to me that entire year. She was grateful when I came and took her out. I saw her show some humility for the first time. Her heart had broken open because her one and only love had left her. She got angry at the other residents of North Park, but she was finally nice to me, and she adored Beth. The last time I saw my mother before her last bout of illness was a perfect evening when Beth, she and I went out for dinner and then to the Parker Playhouse in Ft. Lauderdale to see Mandy Patinkin do a one-man show. He sang many old songs from the 1920s and 1930s, and I could hear her quietly sing along.

During that year, Marshall flew down many times, too. One of those times, right after my grandson Jacob was born, Marshall flew down to Florida, waited until our mother's dialysis treatment was finished, and then drove her down to Key West to meet her first great-grandson. They stayed two days, and he got her back just in time for her next treatment.

HER LAST SURGERY

A week before my mother died she was admitted to an ICU. Marshall and I flew down and met at the Ft. Lauderdale airport. We went straight to the hospital. She was sitting up in bed looking pretty good. She always perked up when she was in the hospital. She became a sweet little girl and loved the way the staff took care of her. And they loved her, too. She was what they considered a "good" patient. They all called her names like "Darlin'."

Marshall and I stood over her not knowing what to say. She finally said, "Well, why are you here? Did you spend a great deal of money on your airfare or did you get a good discount?"

"Mom," I said, "that doesn't matter. You're in ICU, and we've come to be with you. You don't look so good. Let's talk, please."

My mother would always tell me after I was divorced and living alone, "You'd better find someone, and fast, or some day you'll die alone." I've known since my NDE that we can't die alone. Even if there is no other living being there it really doesn't matter because we always have help from the other side. My grandmother, my mother's mother, was there for me when I "died," and I would remind my mother of that. Almost everyone I have interviewed over the past twenty years has had someone, or some kind of divine intelligence, to help them. But when my mother constantly threatened me with the idea of being alone when I died, that was a sure tip-off to me that she was afraid of being alone when she died. Now I wanted to talk with her about that very thing.

"Mom, do you think you are close to dying?"

"I certainly am not," she answered.

"Well," I continued, "if you were, do you think Daddy would come to get you? Or maybe your mother? She came to get me when I almost died. Remember?"

"Yes. I remember and I don't want to talk about it. I'm not dying." And she went on to remind us how angry she was with our father. How could we forget? We had taken her less than a month ago to his grave, and she had cursed him for leaving her.

Just two weeks earlier I had gone to Miami to give a workshop at Unity on the Bay. I brought my mother along. There was *A Course in Miracles* lesson before the regular service, and I was glad we had gotten there early to hear it. The person teaching was talking about forgiveness and the *Course*. Someone came to get us to meet with the minister, Bill Cameron, in his study. My mother wouldn't get up. She was glued to the teacher's every word. I was thrilled to watch her sitting there hearing about forgiveness with a look of questioning and maybe even wonder.

I was asked to give the sermon that Sunday morning. I decided to talk about my life review. I started by saying what a special day it was for me and my mother. I announced that she was here with me and that this was the first time in probably, well, maybe *ever* that we had attended a religious service together (other than weddings, bar mitzvahs and funerals). I pointed to where she was sitting in the front row and the entire congregation applauded. She was beaming. I centered my life review around the idea of forgiveness. I accentuated forgiveness. She was still beaming. I prayed that she'd get it. But from what she was now saying in the hospital, and even worse, from the look on her face, she had still not forgiven our father for leaving and she wouldn't begin to talk with me about her leaving either.

Marshall and I sat and talked afterward about how we spent half our childhood waiting to get into an ICU or regular hospital floor to see our mother.

We went to Beth's to spend the night, and he and I talked and talked about our feelings.

Beth listened and made the most outrageous suggestion:

Why didn't we run down to Key West to see Robin, Steven and Jacob, and she would call us if anything changed for Mom? We jumped at the chance. Marshall and I went to the ICU early the next morning and told our mother we would see her the next evening. Then we were out of there. My brother and I talked all the way down through the Keys—about our children, about our work and about what happened to our childhood friends.

Sitting and listening to Marshall talking with Steven and Robin was an education. All three of them are teachers and they talked nonstop about their jobs. Steve and Robin told Marshall their stories and feelings about teaching, and he could relate them back to his own experiences thirty or so years ago when he started teaching.

I didn't have much to contribute to their conversation, but it didn't matter to them or to me. I got Jacob! I held this baby so tightly and cradled him with a marvelous sense of love. What a grandparent is capable of feeling for a grandchild is way beyond words. I remembered how I felt about my grandmother when I was little. Then in my NDE, I got to feel all of her feelings about me. When she embraced me we melted into one memory. I could still remember all the scenes between us and I could also feel them. We were one and we both loved each other dearly. Now, Jacob reminded me of that special love. I looked deeply into his eyes and said, "Oh, Jacob! The gifts we are going to give each other!" And I so looked forward to our years of sharing unconditional love. Of course, I couldn't keep him in this conversation for more than a few seconds because "Mr. Jako," as Charlie calls him, had learned not only how to crawl since I'd last seen him, but he was also up on his feet and walking around the furniture. Jacob took off across the living room floor. Marshall and Steven were still talking about teaching.

"I know what these kids are capable of. I know their strengths and I know their weaknesses. My problem is that some of them are still trying to see what they can get away with," Steven finished with a sigh.

Marshall was laughing now, and leaning back in the chair, stretching his hands above his head. "I know. Boy, how I know. It doesn't just happen in the beginning. They're always testing until about the eleventh grade and then they settle down. The thing that changes is in *us*. We smooth out at about our third year of teaching, and we just seem to ride over these 'testing' episodes until they smooth out."

Jacob crawled up to me, pulling a book along with him. I pulled him up on my lap and opened the book. He totally relaxed with his back leaning into my chest. This felt so good. As I read him the words of his book I thought about what a good job these two young people were doing raising Jacob. They both work five days a week. Up at the crack of dawn to feed Jacob, grab breakfast, pack lunches and drop Jacob off at day care. Go to work and then pick Jacob up and do a whole evening routine. I remembered what Steve had said at my father's funeral about "Grandpa's work ethic," and I understood a bit more about the wheel of life—the "chains that we don't want to break."

Marshall and I drove back to Ft. Lauderdale on Sunday evening, just in time to make the last five-minute visit in ICU. The nurse told us our mother would be in a regular room the next day and home in a few days.

When we entered her room my mother told us she was sicker. We told her what the staff nurse had said. Her eyes glazed over. That conversation was done. She tried to shame us for going to Key West. I felt ambivalent about the shame and grateful for the time spent with my brother and my kids.

I told her she was going home in a few days. She told me I should stay and take care of her. I said I couldn't stay, but that we were arranging for a home-care nurse to be there around the clock so she wouldn't be alone. We reminded her that she usually rallied, and if she didn't this time, we would keep the nurse on and visit her as often as we could. I told her I loved her. Marshall told her he loved her, and we kissed her good-bye.

As we walked out of the hospital, my life again flashed before my eyes. I could see my mother on gurneys. I could see her in ICUs, being wheeled out of surgery. Body casts, leg casts, braces—you name it—they all danced before my eyes. I had seen them all while attending to her. She had a chronic need to be in the hospital.

On the way back to the airport we had to stop at a gas station to fill up the rental car.

Marshall was pumping gas and I was cleaning out the inside. I'll never forget this scene. I got out of the car and was sobbing. Even though the nurse had said she was better and would go home very soon, I knew in my heart that I would never see my mother alive again.

Marshall looked at me and said, sounding so much like our father that he just about blew me over, "Barbara, you've been alone for too long, and now you have something really good with Charlie. You can't throw it all away to come down here and take care of Mom."

I don't remember what I said to him. I only remember feeling how much he cared for me. How had I missed my relationship with my brother when I was younger? I realized, or I "saw," my brother in a way I never had before. Everything our children had said about our father at the graveside service, my brother showed, too.

My mother went home two days later. Her nurse's name was Sylvia. We all chuckled over the coincidence. The universe was providing my mother with those names again. She spent her childhood with Sylvia and Eileen. Now Sylvia and Eileen were back to help her as this life ended. She had never gotten along with her sister Sylvia. This new Sylvia sounded wonderful over the phone. She babied my mother, being one of those naturally loving people. Eileen checked in on her a few times a day, as did the resident nurse and the social worker.

HER DEATH

Four days later my mother was readmitted to the hospital. I got the call just as Charlie and I were leaving for the airport to fly to Seattle. We were both giving keynote addresses at the American Holistic Medical Association's Annual Convention entitled "The Language of Medicine: Redefining Health and Healing." I got the name of my mother's nurse and called her. Because she didn't know anything yet, I said I would call her again in a few hours, when we landed in Pittsburgh. When I called back, she said my mother had been taken to surgery, opened up and then closed because she was beyond help. Of course, I had heard this before and my mother had always rallied, so I tried to sit on it while we flew to Seattle on the opposite side of the country.

By the time we checked into the hotel and opened the door to our room, the phone was ringing. It was Beth. It was the middle of the night in South Florida. My mother had died. The physician who called Beth waited for her to get there before he unplugged her grandmother from the machine that was breathing for her. Her heart had already stopped, but he did it that way because he was a compassionate person who cared. Kenny, an old school friend who was a respiratory therapist, met Beth at the entrance. He stayed after his shift because he had heard about her grandmother dying. The resident physician not only waited for Beth, but as he unplugged her grandmother, Florence, from the ventilator, he said a prayer. He recited the *Shema,* one of the holiest of Hebrew prayers.

> *Shema Yisrael, Adonai Elohainu,*
> *Adonai Echad.*
> *Baruch shem kavod malchuso*
> *l'olam va-ed.*

In English that means:

> *Hear, O Israel, the Lord our God,*
> *The Lord is One.*
> *Blessed be the name of his glorious Majesty*
> *forever and ever!*

"Mom," Beth said over the phone, "I stayed by the door while the doctor unplugged her and said the *Shema.*"

"That's okay, honey," I answered. "That's okay. He was so kind to wait for you. He sounds like an angel who came in to help release her. She was so afraid of dying alone and she didn't. You were there, and this doctor angel even said a prayer. I'm so grateful to him and relieved for Grandma. Now she can start to heal. How are you doing, sweetheart? Are you okay?"

Beth said she was all right but her voice sounded exhausted.

"I'll be on the first plane I can catch tomorrow morning," I told her. "I'll call you as soon as I know my arrival time. I'll call Uncle Marshall, and you call Steve and Gary. I'll have Uncle Marshall call Aunt Eileen."

"I've made all the calls already, Mom," Beth replied. "I waited to call you last because I knew you hadn't arrived in Seattle yet. I love you, Mom!"

"I love you too, Beth. So much!"

I got back on a plane early the next morning and flew to Ft. Lauderdale. I said prayers over and over thanking Eileen, Sylvia, Beth and an unknown doctor angel for being there for my mother.

GRIEVING

I thought about all the people I had helped die with honesty and openness, in contrast to how I could never talk about anything real with my mother. We never talked about her death. I could never be myself with her. Tears came and I started to grieve.

I talked to God during the seven-hour flight to Florida. I knew from my NDE that God doesn't judge. I sensed from that experience that we are all God's children. But somehow I had to explain my parents' plight in this lifetime. They had terrible trauma in their childhoods. They suffered extreme pain. I asked for them to feel my love. I prayed for their release and for Marshall and me to be able to grieve and go on living.

The next day we buried our mother next to our father. We stayed for two days trying to sit *shiva* in between taking care of everything we had to do.

I flew back to Seattle for the last day of the conference. My talk was the first one in the morning, and I heard myself telling 400 physicians and healthcare providers that my mother had just died. I told them about the physician who had waited for my daughter and then prayed over my mother as he unplugged her. I knew his kindness was now being "caught" by 400 more doctors and nurses. I heard myself say I felt hope for my mother now that she was released and was with God. Then I gave my talk on "Death, Dying and the Near-Death Experience." I received an unexpected and long standing ovation.

Flying home from Seattle to Baltimore, I started grieving for myself. Both my parents were gone. I had never had a childhood. Once I grew up, I spent years healing. My NDE showed me that trying to heal was much better than numbing out or turning around and becoming an abuser myself.

After each of my parents died, I went around and around feeling my pain, letting it go and feeling it again. Grieving is a strange state. It is a process that took hold of me and ran my life. I continued to work. The rest of my time was dictated to me by the grieving process. I realized after a while that I couldn't hurt so much for very long. Crying was intense for about fifteen minutes, and then over. Then I could numb out for a while, or process a memory. These bouts cycled four or five times a day when my father first died, and then stretched out to twice a day, then once a day, and after three or four months I could skip a day.

One night, about nine months after my mother died, and almost two years after my dad's death, I was in bed ready to fall asleep. Perhaps I was already asleep, but it felt like I was awake and looking into the dark, and the darkness was like another dimension:

> *My father was lying down to my upper left. My mother*
>   *wandered in from the right, as her True Self, her soul.*
> *"Where am I?" she asks.*
> *"You have died," I reply.*
> *"Oh. Where's Daddy?"*

"He died, too," I answer. "He is over there."

My mother wanders over to him and puts her arm around his torso and helps him up.

"What are we supposed to do?" she asks.

I answer, "You can go to be with God now."

"We don't know how."

"Follow my prayers." And I pray with all my heart for God to receive my parents.

My parents float away. They are moving with my prayers. And as they do, a terrible stabbing pain— like a knife—comes out of my back at heart level, as if grazing my scapula, and then disappears. I know a part of me has gone with them. I know they are with God. I feel at peace, and I am happy for them.

There was something so different about my mother in this dream. Because it was more real than any dream I had ever had, I questioned whether it *was* a dream—or something more. Similar to my NDE, it had an "other worldly" sense to me. I believe that I was in contact with both my parents' souls and that they were confused, as many souls are after they die. It's not over for them, or us, after we "die." We continue on our journey of exploration and growth.

The only word I can come up with to explain the way my mother came across to me in this experience is "disarmed." All of her wounding and her defensiveness from *this* lifetime had dropped away, and I was clearly seeing her soul, exhausted, but clearly her *authentic self*. What had "fallen away" was what had happened in her childhood. Living in poverty and with a violently ill father, she was likely wounded over and over again. Then he died when she was eleven, so she experienced trauma and abandonment. My mother suffered from chronic

Post-Traumatic Stress Disorder (PTSD).* All her emotional wounding turned into physical pain and addiction. Conventional medicine didn't know how to recognize PTSD back then. We called it "shell shock," believing that only soldiers suffered from it. I always prayed as a child for a doctor who could help my mother, but none did. Some doctors are emerging now in the new field of trauma psychology. For people suffering today like my mother did, there is now hope and help.

My grieving process has lightened up since that dream. I sense that most of my pain over my parents' deaths is over. Occasionally I still grieve for them, for me and for what we missed.

Writing the above, I grieved some more. And through all of this grief work I have learned to let go of trying to control this process. Like my mother in my dream, I am disarmed. I have no defensiveness left against feeling my feelings. I have experientially learned from the loss of my father and mother that we can't control grieving. It is like having a chronic disease. It comes and it goes. But when it flares up—watch out. Listen to it, to its needs. We need to stop doing and just be with it. The more we struggle against it or try to ignore it, the greater the flare-up becomes. This process of grief is a caving in and a letting go and a breaking through to feelings.

Over time I had put a shell around certain feelings—then the feelings had hardened and become more difficult to work through and release. Now when a feeling comes up, if I can just sit and be with it—let it express itself through my body

---

* In response to our increasing knowledge about PTSD and trauma of all sorts, including childhood trauma, some critics have made up the catchy term, "the abuse excuse." While some malingerers and people with anti-social personality disorders may use such an excuse, for most people their experience of the effects of trauma are real.

or my mood—it will eventually transform. Sometimes it becomes tears that dissolve away tension within my body, my mind or my soul. Sometimes the feeling transforms into an insight or revelation. Sometimes it is unintelligible, and if I can just be with it, it will go away.

What am I learning? Mountains of stuff. I needed to grieve for never having a fun childhood. From that I have learned that I need to make space for the fun and joy I deserve. And I needed to grieve for my mother's and father's childhoods being filled with trauma and neglect. I'm learning that there are forces within me that are more powerful than my need to control them. I'm learning to take care of myself because the process of grieving needs to be attended to. And the deeper I go, the more I'm learning that I'm not a very good mother to myself, because I didn't have the healthy mothering I needed as a child from which to learn how to nurture myself. I need to be still and listen closely to that gentle voice within me that is usually drowned out by the noise of my ego and the world outside. I have learned that I need to send myself more love than I ever have before. And, in the deepest part of me—where I am connected to God—I know I have not lost my parents. We are eternal. This body I call Barbara will drop away. But I will still be me.

The process of death triggers a desire to let all of the truth out. Deathbed confessions are always taken seriously. We also need to continue to look at the truth after our loved ones die. As we learned in Sherry's story, fear can give way to love. But love can only find its way on the wings of truth.

FIVE

Unconditional Love:
May Doherty's Story

I met May and Jim Doherty a week after I moved to Connecticut. Their daughter, Mary Ellen, had invited me to stay with her until I found my own place.

I had gone up to Hartford for an International Association for Near-Death Studies (IANDS) board meeting, and while I was there I gave several other talks. I met Mary Ellen after I had given a talk on unconditional love, as NDErs have described it. I will never forget her walking up to the front of the room and handing me a slip of paper with her name, address and phone number.

"Hi. My name is Mary Ellen Layden. I understand you may be coming up here to live. If you do, I would like to invite you to stay with me until you find a place of your own. I have a four-bedroom home and live alone. My children are away at college and I'm divorced." I was grateful for her kindness, and when I moved north to Connecticut in January 1985 to start my work at the university, I moved in with Mary Ellen for about three months.

The Saturday evening after I moved in, Mary Ellen had her parents over for dinner and to meet me.

Mary Doherty, Mary Ellen's mother, immediately insisted that I call her May. She was in her mid-seventies, and her pleasant face and demeanor instantly reminded me of Billie Burke, the actress who had played Glinda, the good witch, in *The Wizard of Oz*. May had a peaches-and-cream complexion and a radiance about her. She laughed lightly and smiled often. We seemed to "recognize" each other soul to soul, in a heartfelt way. Perhaps what we were having was a "future memory" of the dear friendship that lasted for four years, until her death in December of 1988.

May was ageless. People who knew her often spoke of her youthful appearance and loving ways. She freely offered her opinions to me, and as our conversations grew deeper so did our relationship. May touched me deeply, epitomizing the role of a good mother. I watched her loving interchanges with not only her seven children, who were in their forties and fifties, but also with her sons- and daughters-in-law, her grand-children and her great-grandchildren. Everyone loved her in return for her ability to unconditionally love them.

May was married to Judge Doherty, or Jim, as I was instructed to call him, for fifty-two years. He was ten years older than she. A retired superior court judge, who still sat on the bench as a trial referee, Jim carried himself with poise and power. His demeanor resembled that of Frederic March.

That first evening we met, Jim told me stories of cases he had heard and reminisced about his political endeavors in the state of Connecticut as far back as the 1930s. He admitted to me once that before making decisions on many cases, espe-cially divorce cases where children were involved, he would pray. He prayed not only in his judge's chambers, but also on his knees by his bed. Mary Ellen had once asked him if he had ever lost sleep over a case. "No," he answered. "Every night before I go to sleep I close the book on that day, and after I pray I don't look back."

The only reason I did not fall into idolizing them was because they, especially May, had a quiet humility. I heard human stories from her often, about her dismay and exhaustion at raising seven children. She told me that when they moved their seven children from Jim's old house into the big house where they raised them, the neighbors thought a child care center had moved in. She said that when Jim had political dinners to attend, it was often a struggle to pull herself together, dress up and look composed.

"What I really loved doing back then was taking each baby, one at a time, to the window. I would hold them so their cheek was next to mine, and I would take their little hands and point to each thing we saw while telling them its name. I did that every evening and sometimes in the morning. It was the only time I could be alone with each of my children." She told me she didn't regret anything in her life. She would do everything all over again.

She also told me about her survival tactics with such a large family. "In order to survive, now that my family has grown up and grown in numbers—there are now twenty-one and more on the way—I unconditionally love them all, to save me, and to keep my sanity!"

"Wait a minute," I said. "You practice unconditional love to protect yourself? How does that work?"

"Oh, my dear," May answered, "when you have as many children and grandchildren as I do, someone is always in crisis. I can't get involved in any way that will pull me in or I'd always be in crisis. So I unconditionally love them no matter what is happening." She said this with a beautiful smile on her face and with her hands folded peacefully in her lap.

I had just met the first person since my NDE who really knew and lived her life with unconditional love. May was a humble person who believed that living a life of unconditional love was preserving her sanity—and it was. But she was also practicing a method of living that most people are not evolved enough yet to manage.

She asked me about my NDE. I told her all about the unconditional love I had felt from my grandmother in the tunnel and from the being/energy that held me while I reexperienced my life. May nodded, comfortable with the concept of unconditional love and more. She understood and agreed when I told her God didn't judge me. She agreed that there is no judgment. We are unconditionally loved. We do the judging ourselves.

"It really doesn't even feel like judging," I said. "It's more a learning process—why things happened the way they did, and why we acted or reacted in a certain way. In some life reviews, a few NDErs even experience why others in their lives reacted the way they did. And while they were over there, looking back at what happened here, they also realized that there was a cosmic balance within their lives. Everything that had happened in their lifetimes had happened for a reason."

As I finished speaking, I realized Mary Ellen and Jim were quiet. They had been listening, too, and were now smiling at me. I felt myself flush with embarrassment. I could not have had this kind of conversation in the life from which I had just moved away.

May turned to Jim and Mary Ellen and said, "There's a letter written by St. Paul, to the Corinthians, where he talks about an experience that could be a near-death experience. I'm not sure if it's one letter or several letters. He wrote of a man who was taken up to the third heaven." May looked at me and said, "That's the level of paradise where God resides. Paul wrote that he heard words so secret that human lips may not repeat them. He wrote about this experience in the third person but it was him. He had been stoned to death in Lystra some fourteen years before he wrote the letters. He was dragged out of the city and left for dead. His converts found him and formed a circle around him. He came back to life, got to his feet and went back into the city. That must be when his near-death experience happened."

I was intrigued. "Paul's waiting fourteen years before he wrote about his experience is typical of many near-death experiencers. And talking about it in the third person is common too."

May said, "There's one quote of his I love in 2 Cor. 5: 1-2 where he says, 'For we know that if our earthly house, this tent, is destroyed we have a building from God, and a house not made with hands, eternal in the heavens.'"

Jim said, "Paul's experience was so personal that he talked about it like May said, in the third person. But from what I remember, it was the confirmation that he needed for his personal assurance and for his teaching."

I answered, "Yeah. That's one of the big meanings of the NDE, for the experiencer, a personal confirmation and assurance. At first we feel like the experience is ineffable, or what Paul said about hearing words so secret that human lips may not repeat them. Eventually, we realize a personal confirmation which many times turns into a mission or special purpose." It was wonderful for me to talk about NDEs in a relaxed family setting. I hadn't been able to do that before.

Later, as we said good night at the door, Jim put his arms around me and gave me a big kiss. "Wow," I said, then declared to May, "You'd better watch out." Without missing a beat, she retorted with the mettle of a much younger woman, "No, my dear! You'd better watch out!" From that moment on it was no secret that the judge loved me (and I suppose many other women), and May tolerated that in an easy, lighthearted way, because as he once told me, and she did too, he had not wandered from her through all the years they had been married.

EASTER

Easter came and the entire Doherty family gathered at Mary Ellen's. I had just moved into my own apartment but had been invited to Mary Ellen's for Easter. After that, I was included in all the family holidays with Mary Ellen and her parents for the six years I lived in New England. As I was leaving my apartment to join the family and experience my first Irish Catholic Easter, the phone rang. There was a terrible crisis in my family. I was devastated. I walked into Mary Ellen's trying not to reveal my fears, knowing I would be driving to Florida the next day. May walked up to me and made total eye contact. She placed a small soapstone rabbit in my hand. "Rub it!" she quietly demanded. "Whatever is happening will be all right. Rub this little bunny and ask God for help. I'll pray for you, too." I felt suddenly grounded and connected to May at the same time.

I didn't have to tell her or anyone else what was going on. I didn't want to. It was Easter. I clutched the soapstone rabbit, rubbing it when I felt worse. I left for Florida to be with my family the next day. I had the smooth soapstone rabbit in my hand or in my pocket the whole time. I felt connected to May and to her prayers, and the crisis was eventually resolved.

May and Jim were devout Catholics who loved the rituals of the church and found peace in their practice of them. I believe that even without her religious beliefs, May Doherty was in touch with and emanating a spiritual presence. Her personal spirituality was a direct result of the open-hearted and open-minded way she walked through life. May proudly told me she had read all of Shirley MacLaine's books. She had also read Raymond Moody's bestseller, *Life After Life*. And she often asked me about my research.

The Doherty family was not without the same trials and tribulations as most other families. With such a large family they probably had more problems and crises than the average. Even with all those problems the family was held together by these two people who, as they reminded me, had their own ups and downs, flaws and good points, memories to be proud of and some they wanted to forget. But this book is not about people's shadows.

POINTINA

One Sunday afternoon, May called and invited Mary Ellen and me to go out for an early dinner. It was a delightful spring day, the first weekend where we could feel winter was over. Jim drove. As I sat in the back seat, I noticed an eight-track tape player in the dash. "Do you have tapes for that player?" I asked, since I hadn't seen one in a long time.

"Sure!" Jim said. "May, show Barbara how it works," and he chuckled. He seemed to be in a grumpy mood when Mary Ellen and I squeezed into his back seat, but as always, as soon as she or I addressed him, he perked up. Without saying a word, May opened up a case and held up Ella Fitzgerald. The two of us in the back seat exclaimed, "Yes!" and she pushed the huge cassette in. "Gee Baby, Ain't I Good for You?" wailed from the speakers. We drove for an hour down to the Connecticut shore, enjoying the sun as it melted the existing patches of snow on the sides of the rocky hills. The still bare trees seemed to stretch to catch their share of the sunlight. After a long winter's nap, the earth was coming alive again. We sang wonderful old songs with Ella: "It Ain't Necessarily So," "A Fine Romance," "Stompin' at the Savoy," "A Foggy Day," "Summertime," "Cheek to Cheek" and "Can't We Be Friends?"

We ate at a typical New England seafood restaurant specializing in fresh Maine lobster. Having grown up in the Midwest where lobster had to be trucked or flown in, and later living in Florida where we ate Florida "lobster"—not lobster at all, but crayfish—I could appreciate the freshness of this wonderful shellfish. "I am amazed at the freshness of this lobster," I said, as the four of us crunched claws and dunked pieces in melted butter.

"Well, my dear," May leaned over the table to get closer, pretending to tell me a secret. "You can have lobster many times this summer when you come to be our guest here at the shore."

Jim grunted and said, "Maybe, May."

"Yes, dear. But I do have a wonderful place to show the three of you after dinner. That's why we picked this restaurant. So I could show you a home on the beach that we could lease for a month. It's not a cottage. It's a beach house that would accommodate all of us for a wonderful summer visit."

Jim retorted, "The farm could accommodate us just as easily. Barbara, did you know we have a farm in Vermont?"

"No." I barely got my answer out because he ran over it.

"Yes. We bought it when the children were little so we could take them to a place in the summer where there was no traffic. They could play on 155 acres of untouched Vermont land. We have a farmhouse that can easily sleep ten.'"

"Yes," May chimed in. "And it's more than a four-hour ride."

Mary Ellen recalled their visits there with a deep sigh. "We would drive up packed into the old car like sardines. Seven kids and a dog. Dad focused on driving while Mom made sandwiches the whole time. She sat in the front seat spreading mayonnaise and passing sandwiches back. When I was old enough, sometimes they would let me go on the train like my older brother Jim."

"May, why can't we just go to the farm the way we always have?" Jim asked.

"We always go to the farm." She looked directly at me. "I've always loved the water. Jim doesn't care about it but I do. So this time let's do the shore!" Still looking at me I knew her comments were meant for Jim's ears.

After dinner we drove no more than five minutes, turning down a road called "Pointina," and I saw Long Island Sound for the first time. We pulled onto a dirt road leading into a parking lot for about ten cars behind a huge white clapboard home. Jim refused to get out.

"It's too windy. I'll stay in the car," he said with finality, while May looked perplexed. Suddenly, with a glint in her eye, she said, "Well, then pull over to the far side of the house, where you can at least get a view."

Jim pulled the car over to the west side of the house onto the lawn where the scene was incredibly lit up by the setting sun just touching the horizon. It was a huge ball of orange, and we had a perfect unobstructed view of it over the water. Jim pulled up his seat so we could squeeze out. He sat clutching the wheel the entire time we joyously explored the grounds. I remember that orange and pink sunlight bathed the land in its glow. The water was deep blue with silver waves dancing. The sky was deep blue, too, with streaks of orange, pink and purple.

In her pastel dress, lit up by the setting sun, May showed

Mary Ellen and me around. Mary Ellen whispered to me, "Relax, we're just in the middle of a 'May getting Jim to do what she wants' routine. This place is great. Isn't it?"

Having just moved here from south Florida, my eyes and senses were having trouble adjusting. This was the same Atlantic I had known in Florida, the same waves crashing in on the shore. But where were the soft sand beaches? Where was the lush tropical greenery? Spring was just beginning, and other than the trellis and arbor covered with wisteria, and the grass surrounding the house, everything was gray and barren.

Ella Fitzgerald's voice drifted from the car, singing "Heaven, I'm in heaven," The perfect accompaniment as we three women sat for a moment in a white gazebo and surveyed the spectacular 360-degree view. I started thinking about the film *On Golden Pond*. May and Jim were so much like Katharine Hepburn and Henry Fonda in that wonderful movie that had captured America's heart. Then May told us that Katharine Hepburn lived less than a mile up the beach. And Eugene O'Neill had written *Ah, Wilderness!* in a beach house only a mile or two in the other direction. She said Pointina Road was called that because the land ended out on this point where we were sitting.

May pointed to the front of the house, which faced south. The silver-blue water went out to the horizon and was met by the blue evening sky. There was a thin stony beach, too. What she said she loved was the way this house sat on the end of the point. It hung at the edge of human civilization looking out over a sea view that—as one summer became many at Pointina—I realized was the closest view of eternity I have ever witnessed in this reality.

Huge boulders were scattered everywhere in the water and occasionally interrupted the shoreline and touched the seawall.

There was a long man-made pile of boulders jutting from the far corner of the point out into the sea for about 100 to 150 feet. For four years I would watch the Doherty clan test their skills at climbing out to the end of those rocks. I remember doing it only once with my heart in my throat and a tremendous amount of coaxing.

As we walked into the house from the parking area on the north side, there was a butler's pantry and laundry area opening up to a huge, avocado-green, 1960s kitchen. Beyond the kitchen, facing west and the sunset, was a big paneled dining room with a table that could easily seat fourteen or more. Every evening, dinner would include a spectacular view of the setting sun through the huge picture window.

When we walked into the main room of the house, my eyes couldn't take it all in at once. The ceiling had to be twenty feet high. There was a huge fireplace and a pile of wood ready for the cool New England summer evenings. At the far end was a wall of glass opening to a sunken sun room that then looked out on the lawn and sea. Big overstuffed sofas and chairs were scattered everywhere, inviting a large family to lounge and visit. We went upstairs to an incredible outdoor deck. When we stood on it we felt like we were standing on the back of a cruise ship.

May smiled and said, "All of you children who want to sleep over will have to take turns. But we can have our days here with everyone together. There's plenty of room. And you two young women have first pick on dates if you'd like to stay over."

"Wow!" was all I could get out of my mouth, but in my heart it was registering that I was going to experience some summer fun from a perspective I had never known before. And with May more than willing to be *everyone's* mother.

As we strolled back out to the car, Ella was now singing "Let's Call the Whole Thing Off." May leaned softly against the car and said to Jim, "Doesn't that gazebo remind you of 2340?" (That was the home Jim was raised in.)

Mary Ellen and I were out of their sight, and she quietly said to me, "Are you listening to this, Barbara? Mom knows so well how to soften Dad's resistance to any idea."

I chuckled and thought out loud, "She's a master at it. But I guess they've been married long enough that they *both* know what's going on." And we smiled.

Every summer for the next four years, May and Jim rented the big house on the end of Pointina Road. I was always included, and they became the parents I had always wished for. Their children became the big family I had always wanted.

There was something different, though, about the summer of 1988. May had slowed down somewhat. She needed more help than usual. Mary Ellen and I did our share as did the others in helping May and Jim move in for the month.

About eighteen months before she died, May had suffered an allergic reaction. Her physician had given her steroids, which made her face look full. I wondered if she was just getting older and having trouble springing back. She seemed to withdraw more into herself, sat more—sometimes reading—often staring out into the sea. It hit me one day when I tried to speak to her from behind and she didn't answer. I spoke a little louder and she still didn't move. I got in front of her face and said, "May, are you having trouble hearing?"

"Yes," she answered sadly. "I was supposed to be fitted with a hearing aid a while back but I don't want to do it."

My Sony Walkman tape player was in my suitcase. I ran and got it. It had a Mozart concerto in it. "May," I asked, "do you want to use this? You can turn the volume up and hear this wonderful tape."

She said, "Why, Barbara, I don't know. Well, I'll try it."

After that May wore headphones most of the time. We got her more tapes and she would sit in the sunroom when it was windy and on the lawn when it wasn't, staring out at the sea and listening to classical music. She wrote me a beautiful note, thanking me for giving her back music. May was known for her notes. No matter how little or how big an act, May always acknowledged kindness with a handwritten note.

As Mary Ellen and I were driving down after work one Friday for a whole weekend at the shore, I asked her, "Do you think there's something wrong with your mother? She's not looking good."

"Yes," Mary Ellen said with a sigh. "All of us have noticed it. She's not going to the doctor, either. She knows what's going on. She could be dying."

We were quiet for several minutes. Then Mary Ellen said that May's cutting garden was probably in full bloom and no one was there to pick the flowers. If we deviated a bit from our drive to Pointina, we could pass by May and Jim's house. We decided to do it. We changed course and there we were at May's garden, ablaze with color. There were so many flowers we filled the entire back seat of the car. We created flower arrangements all over the beach house. Every room spilled over with color. However, it didn't erase the ache in our hearts.

David, the youngest of the seven, came down for the weekend, too. The three of us "kids" went off exploring the shoreline and promptly forgot about the time and the tide. We walked the thin beaches with sometimes only a foot between the water and the seawall. We talked a little about May's condition but weren't sure about anything. We became absorbed in seagulls, sandpipers and two wonderful snow-white swans. We walked out on a sandbar and got back to shore just in time, or we would have been stranded. The sun was setting in its usual amazing way, with orange, pink and purple lighting up the thin strings of clouds in every part of the sky. It looked like the Hollywood movie set for *The Ten Commandments.* I said I expected to see either Charlton Heston or Moses walk across the water any moment. That made the three of us laugh and get silly as we tried to outdo one another skipping stones. Then David said, "Uh oh! Mary Ellen, we weren't watching the tide. We're stranded." And the three of us howled with laughter. As we edged our way back, clinging to the seawall, we became soaked.

Finally, back at the house, we traipsed across the lawn and convulsed into laughter as we splashed into the sunroom where May and Jim were quietly reading.

May said, "Oh, my goodness! Children, you are dripping on the floor." She tried to hide her smile but couldn't contain it. We tried to tell them what had happened but each time one of us did we would start laughing again. Jim and May were laughing, too, but not as much as we were. We were also freezing.

"Go, go!" she yelled over our laughter. "Go and get dry or you're going to catch your death of cold! Go now and I'll fix you some hot tea."

"No, Mom. Don't do it," we chimed in. "We're going to take us all out for ice cream after we change." And we laughed again at the thought of eating ice cream when we were so wet and cold.

"We're going to take you and Dad out for a treat."

"Oh! Go on with you. The three of you are nuts!" Jim laughed.

And try as we might, they wouldn't go. So we changed and went out to find an ice cream parlor. We brought back big gooey sundaes with chocolate syrup and mounds of whipped cream. Jim and May smiled as they ate theirs. The three of us laughed off and on for the rest of the evening. Occasionally, we could catch May and Jim laughing, too.

I remember hearing the waves crashing loudly against the shore that evening as I curled up in bed. I remember being so grateful for this family.

"DON'T BE AFRAID"

The day I found out Simon and Schuster was offering me a contract for my first book, *Full Circle*, was also the day it was confirmed that May had cancer. She was told she had only a few months to live. She called and told Mary Ellen from the hospital and we drove immediately to see her.

We talked for a few minutes about what the doctors had said and then May wanted to know about the book I was writing. At that time, Pocket Books, a division of Simon and Schuster, wanted to call my book *Don't Be Afraid.**

I told May that Simon and Schuster had offered me a contract, and they wanted the book to be entitled *Don't Be Afraid*. May bolted upright in her hospital bed and said, "Don't be afraid! Don't be afraid! I like it, Barbara. Don't be afraid." Then she looked intently into my eyes and said, "I'm not afraid to die. I'm really not, not at almost eighty years old. But I am afraid to leave Daddy. And I had so much more to do and say with the kids."

---

* I later rejected that title because I wanted the focus to be about transformation, not about losing our fear of death, although that message was in it, too. The book was finally called *Full Circle: The Near-Death Experience and Beyond*.

"Say and do it now, May," I answered. "Now is your chance. Don't be afraid! If you don't do it now, it won't happen in this lifetime. Now is your chance!"

May got a twinkle in her eye. She looked directly into my face, studying me for a second. "I've always held back, held it in. You mean now I can tell everyone what I'm feeling?" A giggle was hiding behind her words.

I said, "You are so tuned in to everyone, May. I watch you. I know you. Your kids can be two hundred miles away or in the same house and you always have a hunch or an outright knowing of what is going on with them.

"You should share what you are feeling. You believe in past lives and future lives. You and I have discussed all that. If you don't share your feelings on issues now, you're going to have to do it next time around! That's what unfinished business is all about.

"Oh, May! You're going to do all right for as long as you have left. And Jim will be okay. I promise you. He has three daughters and four sons and lots of children-in-law. Everyone will help him! Meanwhile, as long as you share what you know in your heart, as long as you share your truth, there will be some good times ahead, mixed in with the sadness of leaving, too. And we'll all be here to surround you with love."

May looked at Mary Ellen and said, "Oh, I will miss you!"

Mary Ellen, choking up, answered, "I know you'll be coming back. I'll look for you in my grandchildren's eyes."

May answered in honesty and with a sigh, "Don't look for a long time. I'm tired!"

Then May focused intently on me again and asked, "How am I going to do this? How am I going to leave and not feel such guilt at leaving all the people I have cared for my entire life?"

"May, it is different over there," I said. "Once you release from here, once you let go of this lifetime, everything changes. Everything seems or is perfect. As you journey through to the Light, worries fall away, and it feels like everyone and everything is all right. It is all perfect, even though we don't understand it here."

And then I asked May if she wanted some relief from the stress she was feeling. I'll always remember her face as she nodded, and I told her about the breathing. She looked so sweet as she focused on her breath. I coached her to take an in-breath through the nostrils, breathing in as deeply as she could, and then take an out-breath through pursed lips, as if she was slowly blowing through a straw. While May practiced conscious breathing, I maintained eye contact and breathed along with her, chanting, "Breathing in peace, breathing out stress."

Many weeks later, I again worked with May on her breathing. I asked her to take the in-breath all the way down to her toes. Occasionally I would up the pressure on the out-breath by widening my eyes and showing her that when it felt right she could force the out-breath to rid herself of stress and pain. And I gently let her know that this conscious breathing was a way to help herself when she was ready to release from this lifetime. She looked a little startled, but at the same time, she also knew this was a part of the new peace she was receiving.

NO MORE CHEMOTHERAPY

Before the hospital discharged May, her doctors set up a treatment schedule. It consisted of chemotherapy twice a week for a period of time, then a rest for a few weeks and then another round. The doctors made it very clear that there was little hope this could stop the cancer, but it could give her more time here.

Mary Ellen's two sisters, Lynn and Joan, took turns taking May for her chemotherapy. David drove her just once when the two women couldn't. As they were driving, May asked David, "Would you please do me a favor? Talk to Joan, Lynn, and Mary Ellen and tell them I don't want to go to chemotherapy any more. I've lived my life. I have fulfilled all my responsibilities. Now I'm ready for my reward."

And David said, "Okay, Mom. I'll tell them."

May's family honored her request, although it brought home to each member of the family the reality that she was dying. They could no longer hope that chemotherapy might stop the cancer. May and many of us suspected that she was dying, even before the doctor's verdict. While everyone grieved privately, everyone increased their visits in number and quality.

HEALING CIRCLE

I suggested to Mary Ellen that we do a healing circle for May to comfort her and help alleviate pain. Mary Ellen said I should talk to David about it. He had participated in many healing circles and would be the most comfortable with it. People often get confused when I suggest doing a healing circle for a dying loved one. They think that hands-on healings possibly create the possibility of a cure.

"No," I tell them. "Healings can be for comfort, too. We might not be able to heal a body overwhelmed by cancer, but we can ease the pain of the dying person and the sorrow of the ones left behind by creating a ritual where we give energy and love. Something is shared between us—call it Spirit or energy. It really doesn't matter what we call 'it,' and it doesn't even matter if we believe in it. All we need is the intention to want to help. We aren't looking for a cure. But a healing can take place in the soul if people share love."

I had no trouble convincing David and his two children to do a healing circle with me to help May. Mary Kate was a little over three years old at the time and Nate was five.

The family had rented a hospital bed for May, which they placed on the first floor in the den. This way she no longer needed to negotiate the stairs and was close to all the activity in the house. We surrounded May in her hospital bed. Mary Kate stood on a chair, placing her little hands on May's lower abdomen. Nate, standing on a foot stool, held May's shoulder. I placed both my hands softly on the top of May's feet. David held her head, right hand under her neck, left hand over her forehead.

A few feet away, Jim sat reading the newspaper and occasionally he would peek over the corner of the paper and watch us. When we started, I said a prayer out loud to help us get into the loving altered state that prayer facilitates.*

Before I prayed, I noticed that the children had their eyes closed and were already "there." I smiled and thought about how young kids have no trouble with this. They haven't been taught yet to reject this kind of thing as a natural way of helping others.

"Please, may we be instruments of your healing energy," I prayed, "of your love and your oneness." As I said my prayer, I marveled at the beauty of these two children. They had May's peaches-and-cream complexion, and their cherubic faces resembled those in a great master's painting. They stayed in that

---

* In this context, altered state simply refers to a condition of relaxed focus, calm alertness or focused reverie. Attention is focused on one thing or on a narrow band of things. We have a heightened sensitivity to what we are focused on and a decreased awareness of other things in the environment.

state for the entire time, until I ended the circle by saying a prayer of gratitude out loud.

Two minutes into the circle, I could feel the healing energy moving through us. Not only was I aware of it in my hands that were touching May, but the energy's presence saturated the room. Moments later, I opened my eyes and again looked at the children. Then I glanced at May. She looked totally peaceful. So did David. I looked over at Jim, still sitting at a distance, and he was glowing, obviously catching what was happening. I said softly to him, "Jim, come join us."

Jim was still for a few moments and then he answered, "I can't, Barbara. If I joined you, I would do more taking than giving." There was a softness about Jim as he said that. I had the feeling that he must have come to terms with this flaw in his relationship with May a while ago. May opened her eyes for the few moments this exchange lasted. The glint in her eyes said it all. She and Jim had completed their unfinished business. I looked at David, the last to leave home. His hands were placed gently on his mother, his eyes closed as though in gentle prayer. He never acknowledged his father's comment. I sensed that they had just laid to rest much unfinished business in that one moment.

I asked David about it later and he confirmed my impressions with a big grin. "Boy, that was a big moment for both of them. I'm thankful it happened and that I was there to witness it!"

With our eyes closed again, we continued with the healing circle as though nothing had been said. After twenty minutes, I said out loud, "Thank you, Father, for allowing us to be an instrument of your healing energy. Amen." We opened our eyes, and the children instantly ran off to play, never giving the scene a second look. May looked more radiant than I had ever seen her. She looked back at David and said, "Thank you." She looked at me and said, "Thank you." She swung around, obviously free of pain now, and said to Jim, "Thank you to you, too."

A few weeks later, while Joan was straightening up the house for her parents, she found May's reading glasses by the side of Jim's bed upstairs. She went down to May, who was lying in the hospital bed in the den, and said, "Mom, how did your reading glasses get upstairs by Dad's bed. Were you sleeping upstairs with my father?"

"Well, as a matter of fact, I was," said May.

"But I don't understand. You're too weak to get up the stairs. How did you get there?" Joan asked, puzzled.

"Your father carried me," May coyly but proudly answered.

THANKSGIVING

Early in November, David asked May, "How long do you want to be around, Mom?" Do you want to be around for Christmas?"

"No!" she said, lying in her bed and looking at the ceiling. "No."

David asked, "What about Thanksgiving? This is the beginning of November." Staring at the ceiling for another ten seconds, she finally replied, "All right."

Mary Ellen made dinner at May and Jim's house on Thanksgiving Day. With the wonderful aroma of turkey filling the house, Mary Ellen bathed May, fixed her hair and even put on her makeup. Bob Vining, Jim's nephew, came to say goodbye to May. She had adored him and he made her laugh one more time. Then May's brother Buddy came. He had been in a wheelchair for years and rarely went out. It took him forever to get in and out of the car and walk up the steps to say good-bye to his big sister. He had always said that May had been like a second mother to him, always loving and understanding him.

At dinnertime, May sat in a wheelchair at the dining room table. She had served her family in this dining room for thirty-four years and now Mary Ellen and David served her. There was a twinkle in her eye as she placed the napkin in her lap. She tasted a tiny morsel of each dish, saying that was all she wanted. It was surprising she ate at all, since her appetite had disappeared weeks earlier as her abdomen swelled from the cancer. Later, the entire family came for dessert and spent the evening.

BITTERSWEET MEMORIES

May died a few days later, but not before spending one more afternoon filled with family and memories that were sad and loving and amusing.

I was standing by the side of May's hospital bed, trying to do some healing work because she was complaining that her pain pills were no longer working. May was on her side, with her back to me, and she was staring at the wall.

"Can you move around, May, so I can get my hands on your belly?" I asked. May didn't answer. I couldn't see her face, and I wondered if she was sleeping. I angled myself at the foot of her bed and saw her eyes. They were open. "May," I spoke loudly now, in her ear, "What are you looking at?"

"Nothing," she said softly. "Just looking at the wallpaper."

"Are you enjoying it?" I asked.

"No!" she answered. "But there's nothing else to do. I can't move and I can't sleep so I just stare at the wallpaper."

"You know what you need? You need a picture there. A picture you enjoy. What would that be May?"

"Oh! A picture of my kids, I guess. I can't move around to

see them anymore. I need a picture of the children," she said in a faint voice.

Out of nowhere someone found a Polaroid camera. Even though it was the end of November, it was a warm sunny day, and May's seven children assembled by the front door as daughters- and sons-in-law, grandchildren and great-grandchildren looked on. As much as everyone's heart was breaking, everyone looked at the camera and made an effort to smile. The picture was ready three minutes later. Seeing that it had been my idea, I had the honor of taping the picture on the wall in front of May's eyes.

"Well, what do you think of this picture?" I asked her. She was silent for a few seconds, and then she answered, "That's not the color I told the painter to make the front door. It's too red. I told him to add more orange. It's supposed to be bitter-sweet orange."

By her voice, I could tell that May was becoming upset.

"May, wait. Don't get upset. All the kids are here. We'll think of something."

Pandemonium spread through the large old house and spilled out onto the front lawn, where some of the family were enjoying the warmth of the sun.

"Okay!" I announced to the family who had assembled again. "Guess what, everyone? May says the door is painted the wrong color." I felt like I had a "scoop." In every large family someone gets the scoop first and then announces it to everyone else—sort of like when one newspaper beats every-one else out. All attention turned to the front door. "It's red. What's wrong with that?" chimed the group.

"It's supposed to be bittersweet orange!" I said.

I don't remember where it came from, but within a matter of a few minutes, someone produced a can of bittersweet orange paint. The stick that was dipped into the paint to stir it was taken to show May. We waited a few moments and then, I think it was Johnny, here from his home in Vermont, who came out to announce, "It's the right shade of bittersweet," and we all cheered. The door was painted in a short time and again the Polaroid camera came out. We repeated the picture. Three minutes later, I was taping the picture to the wall in front of May.

"That's it," she said approvingly. "Now that's bittersweet!"

MAY'S DEATH

May died three days after Thanksgiving. She had made one last phone call to Mary Ellen. Joan dialed. All May said was, "Thank you for everything." Those were her last words. It was early in the morning. Joan, Lynn and David surrounded May in her bed in the den. As they studied her breathing, Lynn knew to go upstairs and wake her father tenderly, saying, "Dad, it's time. Get dressed and come downstairs." He dressed quickly and walked down the stairs, feet like lead. Jim knelt beside the bed and looked in May's eyes as she looked at him. They didn't say a word. They just continued to look at each other for a few more moments.

She was breathing loudly, forcing each breath in and pushing each breath out. Jim got up with tears in his eyes, walked into the other room and began to wind the old grandfather clock. He had stopped it a few weeks before because May couldn't stand the sound of the ticking. As he advanced the clock, it chimed over and over at every quarter hour, half hour and hour. The chimes rang out like the bells of a cathedral on a sacred and cherished day. As the clock chimed, May's children chanted prayers and gave her the encouragement to let go—or what David later called a "pep rally."

"Let go, Mom."

"Now you're going on a long, long journey, and we'll see you again someday."

"Look for the Light, Mom. Now you're going to go into the Light."

Joan, Lynn and David maintained eye contact with May as they prayed and she breathed her final breaths in and out. They were all crying as they took turns praying out loud. Finally, David recited words of the New Testament, from Revelation: "Maranatha!" and "Come, Lord Jesus."

May had taken her last breath.

DAVID REMEMBERS

David told me later that he could see May's life leave her body, yet her body still glowed. "There was something almost like a silvery halo around her body," he said. "I wouldn't call it a 'halo,' because I don't see halos, but there was such an aura of tranquillity in all her features, and her skin had become more translucent. It was as though there was a light still there. I kept coming back into the den to look at her face and see that light. Her face was so peaceful. The breathing exercises that you coached her in gave her such peace.

"I stood there, looking at my mother's body for about an hour after she died, and I thought she died the way she lived. She was still glowing, with that light coming from her face and surrounding her body."

"Then I went upstairs to see how my dad was doing, and he told me to go to work. He said that I should go do something normal.

"'I don't need you to stay with me,' Dad said. 'This is the first day in a whole new chapter in my life. Go, David. Put in a day's work.'

"'You sure now, Dad?' I asked.

"'Yeah, I'm sure. Go!'

"So I said 'Okay' and left. I drove all the way in silence, a prayerful silence. I was deeply touched by my mother's death. It was as intense a spiritual experience as my son's birth. It felt like the same thing. We're spirit coming and spirit going.

"I left my parents' home full of gratitude and peace. Then, just as I was driving off the highway to get to my Old Saybrook office, I turned on the radio and the song that was playing was an old 1950s hit, "You Are My Special Angel." I just sat in the driveway and cried and cried. About six months later, I was pulling into the same driveway and the same song was playing again. So I figure it's my Mom's and my song!"

At both May's and Jim's funerals, everyone received a memorial card that had this message on the back:

> *To laugh often and much, to win the respect of intelligent people and the affection of children; to earn the appreciation of honest critics and endure the betrayal of false friends; to appreciate beauty; to find the best in others; to leave the world a bit better whether by a healthy child, a garden patch, or a redeemed social condition; to know even one life has breathed easier because you have lived. This is to have succeeded.*
>
> *—Ralph Waldo Emerson*

SIX

Strength:
Jim's Story

*J*im was eighty-nine when May died. He lived for another seven years, doing his best, playing golf often, but missing May terribly.

The Doherty children rented the Pointina beach house one more time, the following year. It was Jim's ninetieth birthday, and they celebrated it together, gathered on the lawn by the sea. No one knew how long Jim would last without May. He still drove a car, and he would visit his staff from the courthouse occasionally, or meet them for meals. A few times, his sons took him up to the farm for long weekends in the summer. In the winter, his daughters would rent a house in Naples, Florida, and take him there for a month. I had moved away from New England, but I came back a few times a year to visit. When I returned, Jim would always take Mary Ellen and me out for dinner. Sometimes we cooked dinner at his house and he helped us.

The last time I saw Jim, he took Mary Ellen and me to his favorite seafood restaurant. Mary Ellen told me that everyone knew him there. As we walked in and he removed his hat, I realized he had gotten smaller and was hunched over. I had to remind myself that he was ninety-six years old. However, the moment he was recognized and someone walked over to greet

145

him, he stood up straight and introduced Mary Ellen and me with his same old charm and a touch of pride. He walked proudly in front of us, twirling his hat in his hand with almost a skip to his stride. As we sat, he smiled widely and his eyes danced. He told me what he thought I would enjoy eating, and the meal was delightful. I asked him about the special dinner and award that his associates at the courthouse had recently given him. He blushed and changed the subject. It was enough for him to be dining with two "young" women.

JIM'S DEATH

A few months before Jim died, David asked him, "Dad, are you afraid of dying?"

Jim answered, "No, no. I'm tired of living. All my friends have gone. I miss your mother a lot. I'm alone a lot. But I'm not afraid of dying. I know what the Lord promised."

Jim went on to explain that the only fear he had was of not dying at home. He wanted control over his death, just as he had tried to maintain control over his life for ninety-six years. He reminded David that he had sat as a superior court judge, and then as a referee until only seven years earlier, when he retired to help May die.

Jim's seven children tried to accommodate his wish to die at home as he weakened and got closer to his death. Jim was becoming more afraid of being taken from his home to die. He made everyone know he was clear about staying in the house.

David reassured him that everybody knew he wanted to die at home. He later told me, "All seven of us knew that. All seven of us were committed to his being home. I even told him at one point that we had two meetings to discuss him staying in the house and that we were going to make sure it happened. And

Dad said, 'No, I don't want you kids meeting together to talk about my death!' I said, 'No, no Dad. What we're trying to do is be sure that you have your wish. And that you are able to stay at home. And we're doing everything we can.'

"First we made arrangements with a medic alert company. They gave him a necklace that had a panic button on it to wear at all times. We all felt better knowing that if he was in any situation where he needed help, he could hit the button and medical help would respond immediately. Then we hired Frances, the daughter of a cousin. She came in mid-morning and stayed with him to mid-afternoon. He wasn't too agreeable about that, but once she started coming, he loved having her there. Then we had a man coming for three hours, from three to six, and he would help Dad get ready for bed. His name was Will and he was from Africa. He gave beautiful bear hugs. He was a really nice man. I'd come over in the evening to visit with them, and sometimes Dad would become cross with me being there, because I could see he enjoyed Will's attention. I could see this arrangement was good for my father."

The evening before Jim died, David and his wife Terry went to visit him.

David later told me, "Dad was unsteady on his feet. I saw him almost fall over and I reached to catch him. He looked startled and got himself over to his chair, hitting the arm and then sliding in. He looked scared. I got down on one knee with my face close in front of him and looked him in the eye. I told him I couldn't leave him like this, but we couldn't stay, so I asked him if I could call my brother Jim. He agreed."

Jim came over and the two of them watched the baseball game on television. Joe, another son who was also a superior court judge, had just left a court dinner meeting in New Haven and had started the one-hour drive to his home in

Waterbury. He passed by his father's house as he always did driving home. About a mile up the road, he put on his brakes and said to himself, "No way. I need to go back and see Dad."

So he went back and watched the baseball game with his father. They even had a few laughs during the game. Afterward, Jim and Joe watched their father walk to bed. They were close behind him with their hands ready to catch him. He was walking even more unsteadily than he had before. But as always, he carried his walker. He was still in control and only had the walker there in case he needed it. He made it to the bed by himself.

When Frances came in the next morning, she was surprised that Jim wasn't sitting at the kitchen table eating his breakfast. She went to his room and found Jim lying in bed. He had died during the night. His necklace, with the panic button, was on the bedside table. He hadn't made any attempt to press the button. Instead, he had placed the necklace where everyone would see it and understand.

Jim had had his last wish. His need was to be at home and remain independent. His children put their needs aside and supported him in his desire to control his life and his death.

David later said, "That's the way he wanted his death to be. He was independent, and we kids respected that to the very end."

This prayer was on the front of Jim's and May's memorial cards, which were given to us at their funerals. I can almost hear the two of them reciting it to each one of us.

An Irish Blessing

May the road rise to meet you.
May the wind be always at your back.
May the sun shine warm upon your face.

May the rains fall soft upon your fields.
And until we meet again,
May God hold you in the hollow of his hand.

SEVEN

Light:
Claire's Story

*A*bout two years before May died, I was visiting the Doherty farm in Northern Vermont. May asked me to visit a dear friend of hers who was in her late seventies and dying of pulmonary fibrosis. Her name was Claire, and she was visiting with her daughter at the farm adjacent to the Dohertys. Claire lived in New Haven, Connecticut, not far from May and Jim—and me—and they had known each other their entire lives. She had had her own restaurant in New Haven for more than thirty years, so everyone in the community knew her. When people found out I helped assist Claire in her dying process, their faces would light up as they told me stories about her and about how much they adored her. Everyone who knew Claire loved her.

As I approached the deck of the large modern farmhouse, I was greeted by a big friendly dog. From the deck I walked into a spacious kitchen where baskets and drying herbs were hung from the ceiling, reminiscent of a layout in *Better Homes and Gardens*. The far end of the kitchen opened into a sitting area, and there, stooped way over to the point of looking at the floor, sat Claire. Her disease had made breathing so difficult that now she had to lean over in that stooped position to compensate. Pulmonary fibrosis slowly turns the lungs to concrete. Expansion and contraction of the lungs become almost impossible toward the end of the disease, and Claire's posture made it obvious that she had reached that point. A home-care nurse stood just a few feet away, Claire's companion wherever she went.

I talked with Claire's daughter briefly, and she explained to me that this was probably her mother's last visit to her farm because travel had become so hard.

As I approached Claire, I realized I had to meet her at her level and not ask her to sit up and look to me. I crouched down on my knees and bent my neck back and around Claire's own bowed head so that we were face to face.

"Hello, Claire. I'm Barbara," I said softly. We had perfect eye contact.

Claire asked, "Who are you? Where are you from?"

As I looked into Claire's eyes, it registered that our souls were looking deeply into each other. I could feel that her energy had become more spirit than human. She was actually in the middle of her transition, but her body was struggling not to let go. The sense I had of her state of consciousness reminded me of my NDE, because time seemed to be stopped and it felt like we were in that eternal space. Claire's body and mind may not have known this, but her soul was deeply in touch with the other reality we call death.

With this sense of Claire, I followed my hunch by asking her in return, "What do you see?"

She looked deeply into my eyes. "I see love," Claire answered, straining to catch her breath and sounding astonished.

"Claire, I have been where there is the love that you see. I have died and come back here to help people who are very sick." I knew she understood. In fact, I felt as though both of us were out of this reality and in the beginning stages of dying.

"I know you can see the love in my eyes, Claire," I went on. "This love is coming from where I've been. This love is waiting for you, too. When your journey in this life ends, there will be a Light filled with this love." And then I was silent, still crouched on the floor and looking up into her face.

"Will you help me?" Claire said quietly, half pleading, half insisting.

"When you are ready, Claire, tell your nurse to call me and I will come. If I am with a dying patient you may have to wait a while. But I will come to you as soon as I can. Is that all right, Claire? I will come right away if I am free, but if I am with someone else will you wait until I can come?" I had to ask her that because I couldn't be on twenty-four-hour notice for her. I might be sitting with someone else, and when I am sitting with someone I want to be there totally for them. I don't want to be worried that someone else who needs me is anxiously waiting for me to come.

Claire gave me a slight nod and said, "When I need you, I will have my nurse call you, and you will come as soon as you can if you are with someone else."

I watched her withdraw back into herself. It was as if a curtain had dropped and she was gone. I pulled back a little and then straightened my body to a full standing position. My neck muscles let me know they weren't happy with what I had just put them through.

I talked with Claire's daughter and her nurse for a few moments. I gave them my phone number and told them what I had just explained to Claire.

Five weeks went by. I thought that Claire had probably already died, and I hoped my short visit had been helpful. I was sitting with another dying patient one Thursday afternoon when the phone rang. It was Claire's nurse.

"Claire says you must come now," the nurse told me.

"I can't," I said. "I am sitting with another dying patient, and I am the only one here. Ask her if she can wait. Ask her if Sunday will be all right."

After a few moments, the nurse returned and told me Claire had said Sunday would be fine.

I arrived late Sunday morning at Claire's other daughter's house in southern Connecticut. She ushered me into a darkened room where Claire sat upright in a hospital bed. I moved close to her face and said, "Hello, Claire. I'm here. What can I do to help you?"

"I can't sleep," she answered. Her voice was raspy and down to a low whisper. "Help me sleep. I can't rest."

Her daughter said, "She's been so restless. She doesn't sleep." And then she left us alone.

I looked around the room to see what I had to work with. There was a hospital bedside table, the kind used for meal trays, pushed into a corner. I took it and wheeled it just in front of Claire's chest and put a pillow on it. I helped Claire move forward just a bit, so she could rest her head and upper shoulders on the pillow. I kicked off my shoes and climbed up on the bed behind Claire, taking a bottle of moisturizer from a nearby dresser. I started spreading lotion on Claire's neck. I loosened the ties of her hospital gown and rubbed her back. I worked the lotion into her shoulders and the tense muscles around her ears and temples. I hadn't even gone to school yet for massage therapy, but skill wasn't what was needed here as much as was the intention to help another. We didn't need to talk. Claire had said enough already. She was tense and needed to sleep. When I finished a few minutes later, she was sleeping softly.

As I washed my hands I said a prayer of gratitude. I remember feeling especially grateful because Claire was able to fall asleep, and that told me that I had helped. I talked for a few moments with her daughter and encouraged her to lightly massage Claire as she needed it. I told her I would return on Tuesday and left.

Claire's daughter called May Doherty a few hours later, and then May called me. An hour and a half after I had left, Claire's daughter went in to check on her mother and discovered she had died peacefully in her sleep. She told May how grateful she was that her mother finally was out of pain, and then she told May that while I was massaging Claire, she had peeked into the darkened room and had seen Claire and me in a ray of golden-white light.

May thanked me again for helping her friend. However, I noticed for several months afterward that when I saw May and reached to take her hand or tried to give her a hug, she would pull back as if she were afraid of my touch. I finally teased her about it, and she laughed with a bit of embarrassment. She said she was still in awe of what Claire's daughter had seen. Then she put her arms around me with a tender hug.

For the remainder of the time I lived in Connecticut, when I would be giving a talk or just out somewhere, someone would come up to me and introduce themselves, saying that they had been a friend of Claire's and had heard that I had helped her die. They would tell me that her name, Claire, meant "light," and that she was light. The stories were always beautiful and made me very glad I had met Claire, if only briefly. And glad I could help her. I will always remember gazing into her eyes and feeling the Light, too.

EIGHT

Knowing:
Sylvia's Story

*S*ylvia was my mother's oldest sister. Because she and my mother never got along, I didn't get to know her well when I was a child. We would see Sylvia and her family only once or twice a year. She and my mother would fight, and then Sylvia would be out of our lives for six months or more. Then they would make up, and we would act like nothing had ever happened and try to be "family" again. But soon she and my mother would be fighting once more.

I finally got to know my Aunt Sylvia during the few years before her death. She was living in south Florida by then, where I had also moved. At the time I was going to school for respiratory therapy and working in hospitals near her home in South Miami Beach. Sylvia had been courageously fighting breast cancer for four years. This was in the late 1970s and people on chemotherapy sometimes died, not from their cancer, but from the aftereffects of treatment. Often, they lost weight rapidly and wasted away. But not my Aunt Sylvia. Wherever she was, whatever she was doing, she had a bag of Oreo cookies with her and she constantly munched. She got chubby during her cancer treatment and laughed about it.

As Sylvia's disease progressed, she seemed to enjoy life even more and have a greater appreciation for everyone. She was also waking up to the beauty around her. She hadn't had an easy life but now she and my uncle could afford to live in South Florida, which she considered to be the most beautiful place in the world. When she awoke each morning she could look out of their condominium window and see the ocean. Every night, she watched the sunset and she raved about the colors. She would take walks and hear people speaking in foreign languages, and she would pretend she was in other countries. She told me about her new appreciation for life between her smiles and laughter.

As the cancer spread to Sylvia's lungs and she began to weaken, her son and daughter-in-law gladly made room for her and my uncle in their home. I would go there often to visit after school or clinical work. Sylvia told me many times how much she loved living there. The house, built in the 1920s, was designed in art deco style. My cousins had noticed every detail of the deco and brought the original beauty back. And my aunt adored her son and daughter-in-law, always telling me how lucky she was to be with them.

One time when I visited, Aunt Sylvia and Uncle Merrill were in the midst of a verbal fight, screaming at each other in shrill voices. I remembered how other couples I had known often seemed to fight more during a catastrophic illness. So I decided to announce my presence in the house by saying loudly, "You two have a strange way of saying 'I love you.'" They suddenly stopped yelling, looked at each other and smiled. And I could see in their eyes the love that they had for each other.

Sylvia turned to me and said, "Want an Oreo?" She extended the bag, and we laughed.

During the last six months of her life, Sylvia was in and out of a palliative care facility, a place that specialized in keeping terminally ill people comfortable and out of pain. I remember the last time I visited her by myself. When I entered her room, a physical therapist had her up and moving with a walker. Her doctor had prescribed this new aide to help her get around without falling. I hadn't seen her out of bed for a long time. Her legs were still strong and she was still beautiful. It was hard to believe that she was only in her mid-sixties and was going to die.

When she got back into bed she was breathless. I was learning so much about respiratory therapy then, I realized that I needed to help her breathe easier. She was a little foggy from all the pain medication she was on so I moved in close to have eye contact with her.

"Aunt Sylvia, we need to slow down your breathing. Look at me," I said in a soft voice, and I started breathing slowly with her. But she couldn't follow me, and with a dash of pain in my heart, I realized she couldn't slow down her breathing because she had no lung tissue left. I could hear it: her breath ended before reaching most parts of her lungs. I hesitated for a few seconds, realizing how inexperienced my skill and knowledge were, and I prayed for guidance and an open heart.

My aunt was almost panting now. Then I had an intuition, and I asked her gently, "Aunt Sylvia, are you afraid?"

She opened her eyes wide with a sudden frantic look and nodded her head.

I asked, "What are you afraid of?"

She answered breathlessly, "I'm afraid I will never leave this hospital."

In the two years I had come to know my aunt, we had never used the "D" word. "Death" was not in Sylvia's vocabulary during her final years. My first rule with catastrophically ill people is this: if they don't use the "D" word, I don't use it either. I want to respect where they are at and wait until they are ready to talk about death. And if they don't want to, I respect that, too. I believe that each of us, with Spirit—or without Spirit, if we so choose—should control our own dying process.

I looked deeply into my aunt's eyes and said to her, "That is a perfectly normal fear, to be afraid that you won't leave here. Probably every patient who is in this hospital is afraid that they won't leave."

"Oh!" she said, looking a little calmer.

"But let me tell you what is wrong here, with your fear," I continued. I put my hand in front of her face and I made the motion of a spiral—small at the bottom but getting bigger and bigger at the top. Her eyes followed my hand as I made the spiral slowly—from bottom to top—several times.

"Our fear starts down here," I said, "as a little thing. But if we don't talk about it, if we hide from our fear or try to pretend it doesn't exist, it gets bigger and bigger. Sometimes it gets bigger than we are. But if you share your fear with me, it will stay small. And you can make room for other things."

Sylvia's breathing was starting to slow down. "I'm scared," she said. "I want to see my kids, and I'm scared I won't see them again. I want to make room for them."

"All right," I responded. "That sounds good. Gene and Lisa are close by. But what about Anne and Howard? Shall I tell them to fly down here tonight?" I asked.

"What day is this?" she asked, struggling to get her orientation back.

"This is Wednesday," I answered.

"No, they don't have to fly down tonight. Let them come on Friday." She sounded calm and deliberate now.

"Aunt Sylvia, I have to ask you this. What about my mother? She is going to want to fly down and see you, too. Do you want her here?" I asked, almost breathless from the weight of the question I had just asked. She and my mother had still never managed to become friends.

"Yeah," Sylvia said. "Bring her and your father here Friday night. I'll see them. But then take them away somewhere. I don't want her here Sunday morning. I want to be alone with my kids Sunday morning." And she smiled.

I realized I was going to have to do some sharp maneuvering with my parents, and my mind went into fast forward. To bring me back to the present, I asked, "What do you want to wear on Sunday morning, Aunt Sylvia?"

She looked concerned as she answered, "My lavender nightgown and robe. They're here, aren't they?"

I went to the dresser and there they were, fresh and nicely folded. I held them up and showed them to her. She smiled again, and a wistful look came over her face. Her voice faded as she said, "Yes, I will wear that on Sunday morning, and my children and Merrill will be here with me."

I could see she was exhausted. I began to stroke her hair. About an inch of it had grown back since her last round of chemotherapy. I made little ringlets around her face. She sighed a few times, obviously loving the touch. I thought about how her mother—my grandmother who had met me in the tunnel during my NDE—used to stroke and curl my hair when I was a child, and it had felt wonderful. *She must have played with Aunt Sylvia's hair, too,* I thought. I continued stroking her hair until I could hear she was in a deep sleep. I kissed my aunt on the forehead as I stood to leave. She had curled up on her side, hugging her pillow. I covered her and whispered, "I'll see you Friday evening." Then I tiptoed out the door.

I went to the nurse's station and told her nurse about the conversation we had just had, and she wrote everything down in Sylvia's chart for the doctor to read when he made rounds. When I went home that evening, I called Michigan and asked my family to fly down Friday afternoon.

On Friday evening I drove my parents to see Aunt Sylvia in the hospital. The encounter between her and my mother was strained. When they were together, there was a coldness about them that is hard to describe. A traumatic childhood that was fraught with cruelty, poverty and sickness had shattered them both. They were a year apart in age and had been forced to share the same clothes—and there wasn't much to share. Because their father had had epilepsy, they were forced to live with his family. Their father's sisters would tell hurtful lies to my aunt and mother about my grandmother. Unfortunately, the only part of my mother's and aunt's childhoods that they could remember with deep feeling was how much they disliked each other and how much they had hurt each other—physically and emotionally. Now I watched these two sisters, who looked so much alike and who were emotionally paralyzed in their relationship because of a painful childhood. I knew it was time to go.

As we were leaving, I told Aunt Sylvia that we were going to do a family weekend at Disney World. My parents had never been there, so they were thrilled to go. Sylvia smiled and told us to have fun. I told her I loved her, and as I bent over and kissed her, I heard her say in a soft voice, "Thank you, Barbara."

My parents and I spent all day Saturday in Disney World. We checked into our hotel in the evening and later sat around a table in the dining room long after our meal was over. My father talked with everyone around us but my mother never spoke—neither during the meal, nor after. Then my ten-year-old son Gary came back from the Magic Kingdom with his older brother and sister and proudly presented my mother with a little porcelain statue of Mickey Mouse. After that, she joined in, holding her treasured gift with a smile.

We went to Disney World again on Sunday morning. When we returned to the hotel around lunchtime, a call was waiting. Sylvia had just died. I called my cousins. They told me that my aunt—in her lavender nightgown, with her three children and her husband surrounding her—slipped quietly into a deep sleep and then died. Just before she died, she told her daughter Anne that her aunt, who had been dead many years, had come to her the evening before and stood at the end of her bed and smiled.

We drove back from Disney World to South Florida in less than four hours. We drove directly to the home of my cousins Gene and Lisa. We visited briefly and heard about the funeral plans. The funeral was going to be back in Michigan, and everyone, including my parents, would fly to Michigan the next morning.

After we left Gene and Lisa's house, my parents were hungry, so we went to Wolfie's, their favorite deli in Florida. *How odd,* I thought, as we sat there waiting for our food. *Sylvia has just died and we are all dry-eyed, waiting for food that will push down whatever feelings we may have.*

The waiter looked at me with penetrating eyes. I will never forget his face. He smiled and, as he leaned over to place my sandwich in front of me, said quietly, "I'm sorry. Whatever it is, I'm sorry." I started to cry. I thanked him as he left the table. I allowed myself to cry throughout our meal. No one else said a word. I felt great sadness at the passing of my aunt and I let it show. I was quietly grateful for those last few years when I was able to be a part of her life. And I was especially grateful for the angel waiter who now stood across the room, and who had allowed me my moment of grief and tears.

Looking back, I realize that my parents were most likely in the earliest stages of grief: shock, denial and numbness. I had been a part of Sylvia's dying and had already begun to grieve before she passed. Besides, there had always been tension, jealousy and envy between my mother and her sister, and it is usually harder to grieve for the loss of a person with whom there is that kind of unresolved pain.

The relationship that my mother and aunt had is, unfortunately, a powerful example of how not sharing feelings or being real with one another can damage people. I believe that we can make an effort in any relationship that is frozen in unresolved pain to share truth—our truth and the other person's truth. And if the other person won't let us in, we have to respect his or her boundaries. But I truly feel that we should always try. My life review revealed that this is the way to truly live.

NOTES ON KNOWING

Aunt Sylvia knew, on a soul level, when she was going to die. Her mind, or ego, did not want to admit it or say it out loud. But her soul was able to let me know. Many times, our souls know what our conscious mind does not want to admit. This is the best reason I can think of as to why I think—and my life review showed—that we should honor our feelings and be real. As we are dying, our soul talks to us through our feelings and intuitions. Our ego tends to fight that authentic information. When we live, honoring our feelings and intuitions, we are living in alignment with our soul. We are being real.

As I have watched people getting ready to die, I have real-ized that the closer they get to their actual deaths, the more in touch they are with their souls. The soul knows when separa-tion from the body is going to happen. So dying people are more likely to know when they are actually going to make their transition if they can put their egos aside and be honest with themselves. People who are willing to assist the dying can help them with this knowing like I did with my aunt.

I told the story of assisting John Loranger in his final passage in my first book, *Full Circle*. John, only in his mid-thirties, was dying of an inoperable brain tumor. It had totally paralyzed him. He was hospitalized in the ICU at the University of Connecticut Hospital. I was called in for a con-sultation and worked with him over a period of time, until he and his family came to the conclusion that he wanted to be unplugged from the ventilator that was sustaining his life. He had lost the ability to talk except for the use of an electronic voice box that he did not like to use. I had gotten used to his garbled speech and could translate for him even without the voice box.

The morning he was to be unplugged, his family and close friends gathered around his bed and said their final good-byes. He was scheduled to be unplugged at 10:00. Twice, in his garbled and weak voice, he said, "They're coming for me at 5:30." His day nurse would correct him when I translated. She would say, "No, no, John. They are unplugging you at 10:00." The second time I translated for John and the nurse said no, he became agitated. I repeated what he had said and I pointed up with my thumb, making sure he could see.

John was disconnected from the ventilator that breathed for him at 10:15 that morning. He was first given an injection which contained a sedative and respiratory depressant. Just before he closed his eyes for the last time in this life, he looked at his best friend and said (I translated), "Save the Porsche. I'm coming back." We watched his vital signs on the monitor next to his bed. They slowly went down and barely stopped. Then they climbed again to a normal heartbeat and breathing rate. Seven hours later, at exactly 5:30 in the afternoon, John Loranger took his last breath on his own and died.

This man, who couldn't move and could barely speak was in touch with his soul. In fact, we could say he was pure soul even before he died, because he had no more distractions from his body and no more demands from his ego other than wanting to find comfort. It may be hard for us to understand because we are still in our bodies, and our minds are often still attached to our egos.

Those who have made the transition from this lifetime into the next reality do not take their bodies or their minds. We are soul after this life ends. Other metaphors for the soul while we are alive are "heart," "True Self" and "child within." Our souls know authentic experience in the moment, something revealed to me in my life review.

Knowing is all about being who we really are. It is about awareness of what is coming up for us moment to moment in the experience of our real self. Knowing is standing in and experiencing the light of our soul.

NINE

Denial:
Three Short Stories

READER/CUSTOMER CARE SURVEY

If you are enjoying this book, please help us serve you better and meet your changing needs by taking a few minutes to complete this survey. Please fold it and drop it in the mail.

As a special **"Thank You"** we'll send you news about new books and a valuable **Gift Certificate!**

PLEASE PRINT   C8C

NAME:_____

ADDRESS: _____

_____

TELEPHONE NUMBER: _____

FAX NUMBER: _____

E-MAIL: _____

WEBSITE: _____

(1) Gender: 1)_____Female 2)_____Male

(2) Age:
1)_____12 or under   5)_____30-39
2)_____13-15   6)_____40-49
3)_____16-19   7)_____50-59
4)_____20-29   8)_____60+

(3) Your Children's Age(s):
Check all that apply.
1)_____6 or Under   3)_____11-14
2)_____7-10   4)_____15-18

(7) Marital Status:
1)_____Married
2)_____Single
3)_____Divorced/Wid.

(8) Was this book
1)_____Purchased for yourself?
2)_____Received as a gift?

(9) How many books do you read a month?
1)_____1   3)_____3
2)_____2   4)_____4+

(10) How did you find out about this book?
Please check ONE.
1)_____Personal Recommendation
2)_____Store Display
3)_____TV/Radio Program
4)_____Bestseller List
5)_____Website
6)_____Advertisement/Article or Book Review
7)_____Catalog or mailing
8)_____Other_____

(11) What FIVE subject areas do you enjoy reading about most?
Rank: 1 (favorite) through 5 (least favorite)
A)_____ Self Development
B)_____ New Age/Alternative Healing
C)_____ Storytelling
D)_____ Spirituality/Inspiration
E)_____ Family and Relationships
F)_____ Health and Nutrition
G)_____ Recovery
H)_____ Business/Professional
I) _____ Entertainment
J)_____ Teen Issues
K)_____ Pets

(16) Where do you purchase most of your books?
Check the top TWO locations.
A)_____ General Bookstore
B)_____ Religious Bookstore
C)_____ Warehouse/Price Club
D)_____ Discount or Other Retail Store
E)_____ Website
F)_____ Book Club/Mail Order

(18) Did you enjoy the stories in this book?
1)_____Almost All
2)_____Few
3)_____Some

(19) What type of magazine do you SUBSCRIBE to?
Check up to FIVE subscription categories.
A)_____ General Inspiration
B)_____ Religious/Devotional
C)_____ Business/Professional
D)_____ World News/Current Events
E)_____ Entertainment
F)_____ Homemaking, Cooking, Crafts
G)_____ Women's Issues
H)_____ Other (please specify) _____

(24) Please indicate your income level
1)_____Student/Retired-fixed income
2)_____Under $25,000
3)_____$25,000-$50,000
4)_____$50,001-$75,000
5)_____$75,001-$100,000
6)_____Over $100,000

TAPE HERE DO NOT STAPLE

FOLD HERE

((25) Do you attend seminars?
1)_____Yes   2)_____No
(26) If you answered yes, what type?
Check all that apply.
1)_____Business/Financial
2)_____Motivational
3)_____Religious/Spiritual
4)_____Job-related
5)_____Family/Relationship issues
(31) Are you:
1) A Parent?_____
2) A Grandparent?_____

Additional comments you would like to make:

_____
_____
_____
_____

UNHEALTHY DENIAL

I was asked to visit a sixty-two-year-old man who was in the hospital with throat cancer. He told me in a whisper that he was finishing another round of chemotherapy and needed a few more days of inpatient care before he could go home. He said he had not been able to hold food down for weeks at a time and was sometimes being fed through a tube or intravenously.

"I know I'm too young to die," he said so softly that I had to lean in close to his face to hear. "My family doesn't believe I'm dying. They won't listen to me. I tell them I'm dying and they keep yelling at me, 'You have to fight, Daddy, fight!'"

"How does that make you feel?" I asked.

"I feel like no one hears me," he answered. "I think the cancer is spreading. I can't talk to anyone. No one hears me."

"I hear you and I'll talk to your family when you want me to." I smiled and made sure we had eye contact. I told him I would return the next day.

I visited every day until he was discharged at the end of the week. Our conversations were always the same except when his family was there. When they were, he said little. They would ask me to convince their father to fight and regain his strength.

I visited him at home once. My sense was that this man was in prison. He was being kept. He had no voice. He sat in his pajamas and watched the scene of wife and daughters scurrying around—continuously busy with the duties of caring for a catastrophically ill loved one.

The last time I saw him, I witnessed his death. In the hospital, hooked up to tubes, he lay in the bed and looked up at me. "I'm going to die now," he mouthed the words more than he whispered them.

"Your family is in the waiting room. What shall I tell them?" I asked.

"Don't tell them anything. I need to die and they won't let me." He strained so I could hear his last words to me. "I need to die now."

I sat down quietly next to his bed. I held his hand for a few seconds or minutes, and then I realized that I had to let it go. He needed to leave. Even my touch was keeping him here. His eyes were closed, and I watched the last bit of life leave his face. It was such a peaceful and humble transition.

I checked in at the nurse's station, and they made the necessary call to a resident who came and confirmed he had died. Then I went into the waiting room and told his family. His daughters and wife started to howl. I closed the door. The four women were screaming about their needs, about their loss. I heard anger over his forty-some-year habit of smoking. I heard anger with the doctors and the way they handled his case. I heard anger with the hospital. I waited until the four of them settled down a little and offered my condolences over their loss. I told them I would visit if they wanted me to and I gave them my card.

I helped them to the door of the hospital and I never heard from them again.

DENIAL IN A NURSING HOME

I was called to a nursing home to help an eighty-five-year-old woman die. She had been there for three years because of senility and deterioration. Her seven children ranging in age from fifty-one to sixty-five sat or stood around her bed. Her husband, still robust for eighty-eight, sat sadly in a chair in the corner.

"My wife has been on her deathbed for over a week now," he told me. "Why did they send for you? There's nothing anyone can do for her. She needs to die."

"May I sit here with you for a little while?" I asked him.

"Yeah," he answered. And he told one of his sons to get me a chair.

I sat with the family for an hour. Each one of the old woman's breaths was loud and labored. Finally, there was a period of about five seconds when she didn't breathe. The daughter who was holding her mother's hand screamed and was then grabbed and pulled back by another sobbing daughter standing behind her. The momentum of this pulled the old woman forward, and she gasped and started to breathe again. I quietly got up and went over to the bed and took the first daughter's hands away from her mother. I held this daughter's hand and rubbed her shoulder.

"We need to let her go now," I said as I looked into the grieving woman's face.

"No, I want my mother," she replied and started to cry.

"I know you do. But your mother needs to go now." I was praying silently while I was talking to her. Two other women in the room began to cry along with her. Their father got up, came over and put his arms around the two of them.

"She's right. It's time to let Mama go. I'll be with her again soon and someday so will you."

The old woman gasped and stopped breathing. A few seconds later she started to breath again and then stopped one more time. I think I was in the room with them for two hours, maybe a little longer, when her breathing finally stopped for the last time. No one pulled on her. No one screamed for her to come back. Her husband stood by her side and said quietly, "I love you. I'll be coming along soon."

By holding back her daughters, her husband and I helped this woman to release. If everyone would have continued calling to her, grabbing her hand or pulling her forward, her dying would have continued much longer. She had to die, regardless of how much her loved ones wanted her to stay.

Sometimes the only thing we can do to assist someone in the dying process is to let go and help the others around us to stand back and let go, too.

HEALTHY DENIAL

A forty-three-year-old man in a deep coma was admitted to the intensive care unit where I worked. He had had a massive coronary, his first. His chart said he was a doctor. As his wife sat by his side, holding his hand, she told me they had three young children. The second day, when I came on my shift, I walked into his cubicle to check on the ventilator that was breathing for him. His wife was there and I asked her, "How long have you been here?"

"Since they brought him in two days ago," she answered. "My mother and father are watching our children."

"Don't you think you need to go home and rest?" I asked. "Besides, it would be good for the children to see and be with you for a while."

"Oh, I can't leave him. I keep talking to him. He has to hear me or I'm afraid he will leave. I have to keep asking him to stay here for me and the children. I'm so afraid he will leave me. I love him so and his children need him." And she had to stop because she started sobbing.

"I agree," I answered. "Even though he is in a coma, it is possible he can hear. And it is good for him to hear your voice. But you need to rest and keep your strength up for your sake and for your children's sake. Besides, when he does come out of this coma, you will need to be strong to take care of him," I reminded her.

"But I have to keep reminding him he has children," she cried. Her saying that reminded me of my children when they were young. I thought of the dinner table every evening and how noisy it was.

"I've got it," I answered. "Get a tape recorder and record the children at the dinner table. I'm sure your dinner table is noisy. Isn't it?"

A smile flashed across her face and she answered, "The noisiest I've ever heard." And she picked up her things, looked back once at her husband and said, "Honey, hold on. I'll be back in a little while." Then she left to record her children's voices.

I checked on him as my shift ended. His condition was the same. His mother was now sitting with him. I asked her how his wife was. She said, "Resting, and I'm sure you'll see her back here tomorrow."

When I walked into his cubicle the next day there was a medium-size boom box taped to the headboard of the bed. There was a sign next to it asking all staff to turn the tape over when one side ended. Flowing from the player was the loud chaotic sound of children's voices and dishes and silverware clanging. Every once in a while an adult voice would come in and ask for something. The tape played continuously for eleven days.

Occasionally I would see his wife, and we would wave or smile. After eleven days of this, he finally awakened. He was transferred out of ICU and to the regular floors about four days later.

His wife came looking for me about a week after that to tell me her husband had just told her that he had been in a tunnel the whole time he was "gone." Sometimes he heard her asking him to come back. But he said what was the most amazing thing was the kids' voices. The whole time he could hear his kids playing and eating and just staying near enough to him that it kept him from going down the tunnel. Finally, he said, he followed his children's voices back here.

The wife came back to see me one more time a few days later. She told me she was taking him home.

I included this last story because it shows that denial can be healthy and can lead to a positive outcome. Of course, when there is hope, denial keeps us going. The woman in the last story was much better off for her own sake and everyone around her believing that her husband was coming back.

This happened in the late 1970s, and back then no one talked about people in comas being able to hear. We now know that people can hear while asleep, under anesthesia or in coma, but to what degree they hear is never possible to know.

Denial can be harmful when there is a strong possibility that dying is inevitable. If the dying person or their loved ones refuse to accept the most likely outcome, they are missing their last opportunity in this lifetime to share this important final passage.

EPILOGUE

*S*omeone told me a story about a man who had been watching a butterfly struggling to get out of its cocoon. The man watched a while and then became concerned for the butterfly because it didn't seem to be freeing itself. He got a handsaw and sawed down the limb to which the cocoon was attached. Then he brought the cocoon into the house, took a small pair of scissors and carefully opened it to help the butterfly free itself more easily. The butterfly freed itself and fluttered for a time and then fell to the floor. It fluttered again and rested, then fluttered some more. Finally, it stopped. It had died. Upset over what he had just witnessed, the man started doing research on the life of a butterfly. What he learned was that the butterfly needs to struggle for a long time to get out of its cocoon. In the struggle, hormones are produced that strengthen the wings for flight. Without the long struggle, the butterfly's wings will never become strong enough to support it, and it will soon die.

So, too, our lives can be full of struggle. But without the struggle, perhaps we couldn't survive, learn to fully live and grow to our potential. Our struggle in life is to move toward selfhood—to become all that we are. Selfhood is our butterfly state. This can also mean that we are in alignment with our soul. Our potential self is our soul.

THE EGO

At the beginning of this book I quoted from a poem I had written just after my NDE. I wrote:

The only real pain
When we die
Is if we do it
Without living first.

"Not living first" means not becoming the butterfly or not achieving selfhood. Selfhood happens when we realize our real self and let go of our ego.* Some people never achieve this. Others are able to just before they die. It is as though there is a built-in mechanism that allows this process to happen quickly if this life is about to end. We know it is happening when the dying person is honest and lives every last day or minute being real—living their truth. This connects them to God. There may even be a visible radiance as they align or are already aligned with their soul.

Perhaps I was able to isolate and name this mechanism when I wrote a few times in these stories about people becoming more spiritual than physical. In Sherry's story we could feel her energy was more spiritual than physical. In Claire's story, too, she was closer to the reality I had known in my NDE than this physical reality. Perhaps, then, the closer we get to completing this lifetime, if we are willing and honest, the more we can let go of our ego and align with our True Self. Having witnessed this mechanism happening, perhaps

---

* Ego, here, means a belief that we are separate from others and God and that we are completely on our own. See the appendix for a more thorough explanation.

deathbed confessions are the final example in this lifetime of a soul struggling to come into alignment.

In my NDE, I realized as my grandmother held me that my belief systems had been messed up, and that the reality I was in with her was the real reality. At that moment, I released what I called "a load of toxic pain." That was my ego being released, and now I was my True Self or soul. In the dream about my parents after they died, I said that my mother was "disarmed." I was seeing my mother's soul without her ego which had kept her wrapped in pain most of her life.

Our ego dies with our body. As we assist someone in the dying process, or as we die ourselves, this process of the ego falling away and our becoming real can happen if we encourage it. And, if we are willing, we can start the process now (if we haven't started it already) without being near death. The sooner we realize that we are not our egos, the sooner we can start to live.

Those who are fortunate and achieve this selfhood at an early age have the opportunity to be authentic and reach their potential. They are standing in the light of their soul while they are alive and thriving. They have every opportunity to be truthful and live, so that there won't be that pain of never having lived as they leave this lifetime.

I have found that assisting someone's final passage has allowed me—and them—substantial growth because of the realness and the truth that we share. For everyone who reads this book—if you haven't started to awaken and live more authentically—I hope that you will consider doing it now. Remember the butterfly. You may need to struggle to pull out of the cocoon of the ego, but the struggle can be worth it. The struggle will strengthen your wings, and you will escape the confines of your ego and become the butterfly of selfhood.

OUR SPIRIT

I realized when I almost died, and also when I have experienced the final passage of another, that we don't end at our skin. Our energy fields overlap with the others in our lives. As I said in my own story, we are all connected in a huge dance of consciousness. We are each a part of this consciousness we call God. So we are not just human. We are Spirit. We were Spirit before we came into this lifetime. We are all struggling spirits now, trying to get "being human" right. And when we finish our journey in this lifetime, we will be pure Spirit again.

I refer to Spirit here as a bridge of conscious energy between each of us and God, each of us with each other and each of us with our self. This energy—referred to in the East as Kundalini, Chi, and Ki, among others, and in the West as Holy Spirit, Great Spirit, and Ruach Ha Kodesh, among still others—is always in us and surrounding us, waiting for a request for help in our growth. It wants to be our partner in our path to selfhood whether we have five minutes left to live or fifty years. We could never ask too early—or too late.

Spirit can show itself and communicate with us in many ways, including some of our own intuitions, gut feelings, profound dreams and synchronicities. Synchronicities are linking coincidences that happen often enough to make us realize that our lives are woven from a higher awareness. Examples of synchronicity include thinking of something and at the same exact moment hearing the words of a song on the radio that answer our thoughts; articles or books that happen to fall into our hands at the right moment; a chance meeting with someone who later turns out to be a meaningful messenger or friend; or even the words of people passing by and talking to someone else that answer our questions. There is usually a sense of joy connected to synchronicities. In fact, almost always, joy seems to accompany Spirit when we sense it.

OUR SOURCE

In my life review, I felt God's memories of the scenes in my life through God's eyes. I could sense its divine intelligence and it was astonishing. It loves us and wants us to learn about life and wake up to what is important. I realized that God wants us to know that the only real pain we experience when we die is if we die without living first. And the way to really live is to give love. We are here to learn to love, not to withhold it. But only when we heal enough to be real—when we are in alignment with our heart, soul or True Self—can we understand and give love the way love was meant to be given: without any demands in return. We can do this only when we have learned to release our egos, making us emotionally healthy and real.

When God held me in my life review and we merged into one, I remember this feeling as being limitless. God is limitless. God's capacity to love is never-ending. God's love for us never changes no matter how we are. God doesn't judge us either. During our life review, we judge ourselves when we feel the pain we have created in other's lives. And if we are not emotionally healthy, we judge and attack ourselves while we are alive. I never saw an old man with a white beard sitting in judgment of me. I only felt limitless divine love.

God has no form in the physical human sense. It is only our egos that want to envision God as a human. God has no body and no ego. It is our egos that needs a form like an old man. It is our egos that need to think we will be judged or even attacked by something that powerful. God, as I felt God, and as the others I have interviewed during near-death research felt God, only gives. God interjected love into all the scenes of my life to show me God's reality. And the most amazing part of all was that God held nothing back. I understood all that God understood. God let me in. God shared all of Godself with me—all the qualities, gentleness, openness and gifts, including power and peace. I never knew that much loving intelligence and freedom could exist. I am back here in a body now, with a mind that is boggled as I try to explain this most noble Being that held me over twenty years ago in Earth time. But I also know that God held me in eternity, and I know I will go there again. And so will you.

Most of the people whose stories I told in this book knew they were going back to be in eternity with our God Source. I believe that those who denied that possibility are now there, too. They have all united with our Source. Remember my mother in my dream of my parents? She asked me, "Where am I?"

"You have died," I answered, and then I told her that my father had died, too, and I showed her where he was. My mother then asked me, "What are we supposed to do?"

"You can go and be with God now," I responded.

"We don't know how."

"Follow my prayers," I replied. And I prayed with all my heart for God to receive my parents. I watched my parents moving with my prayers and I knew they were home.

I am here in time, but still with God. It is just a little harder for me to realize God's presence because this body and this ego/mind get in the way. But that's all right. I still feel it. Especially when I am helping someone else make their final passage. I got closer to God when I witnessed May Doherty's unconditional love, Jim's strength, Sherry's forgiveness, my father's loyalty, my Aunt Sylvia's knowing and Claire's light.

I may have even felt God in my mother's woundedness. Every time I prayed for her to heal, I learned more about how to let go and let her live and die according to her own terms. She gave me a struggle that strengthened my wings like a butterfly's.

Being numb or real is a choice we each can make. If we choose being real, then we can awaken and live. And our struggles will all be worth it. I hope that this book has helped you to make your own choice, if you haven't already done so. And I wish you the best in your journey of life and, ultimately, in your own final passage home.

The glory of God is the human person fully alive.

—*Irenaeus of Lyons*

Appendix

WHO AM I?
A MAP OF THE MIND

Charles L. Whitfield, M.D.

Throughout the struggle of the human condition, many people have asked some important questions: Who am I? What am I doing here? Where am I going? How can I get any peace? While the answers to these questions remain a divine mystery, I have found it useful to construct a map of the mind or psyche to begin to answer them. And while the map is not the territory, maps can be useful.

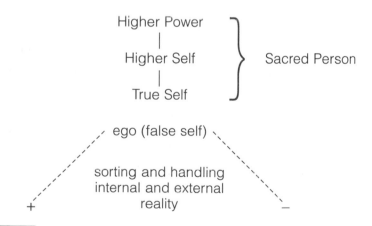

Modified from the foreword in *Spiritual Awakenings: Insights of the Near-Death Experience and Other Doorways to Our Soul,* by Barbara Harris Whitfield, Health Communications, Inc., 1995.

Other names for the True Self, who I really am, include the real or existential self, the human heart, the soul and the child within. They are all the same because they are our true identity. I also have within me a divine nature, sometimes called guardian angel, Atman, Buddha nature, Christ consciousness, higher self, or simply self. And both of these, my True Self and my higher self, are intimately connected to my higher power, God/Goddess/all-that-is, a part of which is also within me.

I see this relationship—True Self, higher self and higher power—as being such an important relationship that I can also view it as being one person, which I call the sacred person. Spirit pervades all aspects of the sacred person.

As a part of the mystery, my True Self makes or constructs an assistant to help me as I live out the human experience. We can call this assistant, this sidekick, the ego—also known as the false self. When this ego is helpful to us, such as in screening, sorting and handling many aspects of our internal and external reality, we can call it positive ego. But when it tries to take over and run our life, it becomes negative ego.

This map of the psyche is more evolved than the maps of Freud, Jung and their colleagues of up to 100 years ago, when they used the term "ego" to mean both True Self and false self. Since the 1930s we have begun to make this more precise differentiation between True Self and false self, and today we use "ego" synonymously with false self.

A contemporary holy book called *A Course in Miracles* says the following in its introduction:

> *What is real cannot be threatened.*
> *What is unreal does not exist.*
> *Herein lies the peace of God.*

What is real is God and God's world, that of the sacred person. The ego and its world are not real, and therefore, in the grand scheme of the mystery, do not exist. Herein, when we make this differentiation, lies our peace and serenity.

But growing up in a dysfunctional family and dysfunctional society of origin, we may have become wounded. That wounding made our child within, our True Self, go into hiding, and the only one left to run the show of our life was our ego. And since it is not competent to run our lives, we often end up feeling confused and hurt.

The way out is to begin to differentiate between identifying with my True Self and my false self, and to heal my wounds around all of what happened to hurt and confuse me. That is what I have described in my books.

While all of this information is useful to know on a cognitive level, it is *healing* only on an experiential level. To heal, I have to experience working through my pain as well as living and enjoying my life.

Bibliography

Bentov, I. *Stalking the Wild Pendulum: On the Mechanics of Consciousness.* Rochester, Vt.: Inner Traditions, 1977.

Bentov, I with M. Bentov. *A Cosmic Book on the Mechanics of Creation.* New York: E.P. Dutton, 1982.

Cohen, C., and J Heiney. *Daddy's Promise.* Bloomfield Hills, Mich.: Promise Publications, 1997. This book is for children and is available by calling the author directly at 248-865-9345.

A Course in Miracles. Tiburon, Calif.: Foundation for Inner Peace, 1975. New York: Viking/The Penguin Group, 1996.

Dossey, L. *Beyond Illness.* Boulder, Colo.: Shambhala, 1984.

———. *Recovering the Soul.* New York: Bantam, 1989.

———. *Space, Time and Medicine.* Boulder, Colo.: Shambhala, 1982.

Goldman, L. *Life and Loss: A Guide to Help Grieving Children.* Muncie, Ind.: Accelerated Development, 1994. This book is for adults helping children and is available by calling the publisher directly at 800-222-1166.

Gordon, R. *Your Healing Hands.* Santa Cruz, Calif.: Unity Press, 1979.

Greenwell, B. *Energies of Transformation: A Guide to the Kundalini Process.* Cupertino, Calif.: Shakti River Press/Transpersonal Learning Services, 1990.

Greyson, B. "Near-Death Experiences and the Physio-Kundalini Syndrome." *Journal of Religion & Health* 32, no. 4 (winter 1993): 277–89.

———. Scientific commentary in B. Harris and L. Bascom, *Full Circle: The Near-Death Experience and Beyond.* New York: Pocket Books, 1990.

193

Greyson, B. and B. Harris, eds. "Clinical Approaches to the NDEr." *Journal of Near-Death Studies* 6, no. 1 (fall 1987): 41–52.

————. "Counseling the Near-Death Experiencer." In *Spiritual Emergency: When Personal Transformation Becomes a Crisis.* Los Angeles: J. P. Tarcher, 1989: 199–210.

Harris, B. "Kundalini and Healing in the West." *Journal of Near-Death Studies* 13, no. 2 (winter 1994): 75–79.

Harris, B. and L. Bascom. *Full Circle: The Near-Death Experience and Beyond.* New York: Pocket Books, 1990.

Keen, S. *The Passionate Life.* San Francisco: Harper and Row, 1983.

Keyes, K. *Handbook to Higher Consciousness.* Marina Del Rey, Calif.: Living Love Center, 1975.

Kunz, D. *Spiritual Aspects of the Healing Arts.* Wheaton, Ill.: Theosophical Publishing House, 1985.

May, G. *The Awakened Heart.* San Francisco: Harper San Francisco, 1991.

Moss, R. *The Black Butterfly.* Millbrae, Calif.: Celestial Arts, 1986.

————. *The I That Is We.* Millbrae, Calif.: Celestial Arts, 1988.

Nouwen, H. J. *Life of the Beloved.* New York: Crossroads, 1993.

Powell, J. *Unconditional Love.* Allen, Tex.: Argus Communications, 1978.

Ring, K. *Heading Toward Omega.* New York: Morrow, 1984.

Sannella, L. *Kundalini: Psychosis or Transcendence.* Lower Lake, Calif.: Integral Publishing, 1987.

Siegel, B. *Love, Medicine and Miracles.* New York: Harper and Row, 1986.

Trout, S. *Born to Serve: The Evolution of the Soul Through Service.* Alexandria, Va.: Three Roses Press, 1997.

Walsch, N. *Conversations with God.* New York: The Putnam Publishing Group, 1996.

————. *Conversations with God: Book Two.* New York: The Putnam Publishing Group, 1997.

Walsh, R. and F. Vaughn, eds. *Beyond Ego.* Los Angeles: J. P. Tarcher, 1980.

————. *Paths Beyond Ego.* Los Angeles: J. P. Tarcher, 1993.

Weil, A. *The Natural Mind.* New York: Houghton Mifflin Co., 1972.

Welwood, J., ed. *Awakening the Heart.* Boulder, Colo.: Shambhala, New Science Library, 1983.

Welwood, J. "The Healing Power of Unconditional Presence." *Quest* 5, no. 4 (winter 1992): 35–40.

Whitfield, B. H. *Spiritual Awakenings: Insights of the Near-Death Experience and Other Doorways to Our Soul.* Deerfield Beach, Fla.: Health Communications, Inc., 1995.

Whitfield, C. *Co-dependence: Healing the Human Condition.* Deerfield Beach, Fla.: Health Communications, Inc., 1991.

————. *A Gift to Myself.* Deerfield Beach, Fla.: Health Communications, Inc., 1990.

————. *Healing the Child Within.* Deerfield Beach, Fla.: Health Communications, Inc., 1987.

————. *Memory and Abuse: Remembering and Healing the Effects of Trauma.* Deerfield Beach, Fla.: Health Communications, Inc., 1995.

Zukav, G. *The Dancing Wu Li Masters.* New York: Quill, 1979.

————. *Seat of the Soul.* New York: Simon and Schuster, 1989.

Index

About the Author

Barbara Harris Whitfield is the author of many published articles and two books, *Full Circle: The Near-Death Experience and Beyond* (Pocket Books, 1990) and *Spiritual Awakenings: Insights of the Near-Death Experience and other Doorways to Our Soul* (Health Communications, Inc., 1995).

She is a thanatologist (thanatology is the study of death and dying), workshop presenter, near-death experiencer and therapist in private practice in Atlanta, Georgia. She is presently on the faculty of Rutgers University's Summer School of Alcohol and Drug Studies, where she teaches two classes: "Feelings, Affect and Emotions in Recovery" and "The Spiritual Psychology of *A Course in Miracles.*"

Barbara spent six years researching the aftereffects of the near-death experience (NDE) at the University of Connecticut Medical School. She is also a member of the executive board of the Kundalini Research Network and has sat on the executive board of the International Association for Near-Death Studies. She is a consulting editor and contributor for the *Journal of Near-Death Studies.*

Barbara has been a guest on major television talk shows including *Larry King Live, The Today Show, Unsolved Mysteries, Donahue, Good Morning America, Oprah, Joan Rivers, CNN*

Medical News, Man Alive, and others. Her story and her
research have appeared in documentaries in Canada, Japan,
Germany, France, Belgium and Italy—and magazines such as
*Redbook, Woman's World, McCall's, Psychology Today, Maclean's,
Common Boundary* and *Reader's Digest.* An interview with
Barbara on her cutting-edge research appeared in Deepak
Chopra's first newsletter, *Infinite Possibilities: For Body, Mind
and Soul,* in October 1996.

Barbara is a respiratory therapist and massage therapist who
works with people who are seeking to integrate and expand
their spiritual experiences. As part of this work she has helped
terminally ill patients die and has assisted family members and
friends in their grieving process. Her interest in this area began
in 1975 when, after spinal surgery, she had two profound
near-death experiences. Wanting answers to what had happened and feeling a "sense of mission," Barbara went back to
school to pursue a healthcare career. She graduated as a respiratory therapist and practiced in hospital critical care units
and emergency rooms, often hearing descriptions of the dying
process and near-death experiences from her patients. She
also found it easy to relate to the friends and relatives of dying
patients and to assist them in their grieving processes and also
in their abilities to relate to each other before being separated
by death.

After meeting University of Connecticut psychology professor Kenneth Ring, and working with him toward an understanding of the NDE phenomenon, Barbara became a prime
subject in his book, *Heading Toward Omega: In Search of the
Meaning of the Near-Death Experience* (Morrow, 1984).

Barbara then founded and facilitated several support groups
in Florida for near-death experiencers and the terminally ill.
She continued facilitating support groups in Connecticut

during her six years of research assisting psychiatry professor Bruce Greyson at the University of Connecticut Medical School. This research was dedicated to the aftereffects of the near-death experience and psychospiritual openings in general. One of the outstanding aftereffects is the loss of fear of death and the desire to help others as they die. Also primary to this research was the "bioenergetic shift" described by experiencers. This shift became what Greyson, Whitfield and Ring now refer to as the "Physio-Kundalini Syndrome."

Barbara continued this research on the bioenergetic changes of spiritual openings by pursuing an education as a certified massage therapist, specializing in several types of Eastern medical models.

Dr. Greyson and Ms. Whitfield then coauthored a groundbreaking paper for the *Journal of Near-Death Studies,* "Clinical Approaches to the Near-Death Experiencer." This paper has been reprinted or quoted in numerous books and articles, including several quotes for the *Diagnostic and Statistical Manual of Mental Disorders IV* (DSM-IV) proposal on "Spiritual Problems."

Barbara continues to study and teach about the energetic shifts inherent to all living beings (information missing from Western science) as a member of the Kundalini Research Network, a group of physicians, clinicians and academicians dedicated to bringing this Eastern science to Western medicine.

Barbara presents workshops and lectures to the public and to hospices, hospitals, massage therapy schools and universities throughout the United States and Canada. These workshops break new ground, helping attendees to expand their beliefs so they can bring their higher nature into everyday life. Barbara offers a new paradigm in healthcare that complements traditional Western psychology and medicine. This paradigm

incorporates a variety of body-based and psychological thera-
pies which validate the role of the True Self in health, whole-
ness and the dying process.

Barbara resides in Atlanta with her husband, Charles L.
Whitfield, M.D., who is the author of five books, including the
bestselling *Healing the Child Within.* You can contact Barbara
by sending a SASE to: P.O. Box 420487, Atlanta, GA 30342,
or email her at c-bwhit@mindspring.com.

For the location of a hospice near you, call the National
Hospice Organization at 800-658-8898.